D1515730

Patriot Fire Team

Manual

Paul G. Markel

?

Patriot Fire Team

Manual

Paul G. Markel © 2016

All Rights Reserved

PFT: Team Manual Contents

Patriot Fire Team; Preserving the Republic Four
Men at a Time   2nd Edition

⍰

Thanks and Acknowledgements

I want to thank and acknowledge those who helped make the PFT Manual a reality.

Master Sergeant (Retired) Shane Iversen, U.S. Army Special Forces and James Yeager MFCEO of Tactical Response both were kind enough to lend me some of their experience and knowledge to share with you within these pages. These men are professional trainers whose schools and courses I highly recommend.

Thank you to Jarrad and Zachary Markel for taking care of the day to day business at Student of the Gun University so that I would have the time to sit down and assemble this book.

A mere "thank you" is not enough for my bride and compass, Nancy Markel. My partner and collaborator for the last three decades, Ms. Nancy knows how to keep me on track and shows me the way even when I cannot see it. Nancy has spent innumerable hours proof-reading, not only this book but several others that came before it. Yes, even Hemingway had an editor.

Team Manual

Foreword

The idea and concept of the Patriot Fire Team is a couple of years old at this writing. We started with an outline that became a "free report" on the www.PatriotFireTeam.com website.

A natural outcome of the PFT idea was the first book, "Patriot Fire Team, Preserving the Republic Four Men at a Time." That book was well received, but it was only a beginning. What will follow in this book is a more detailed and thorough manual that not only addresses the why, but the what and how of being a member of a Fire Team.

Again, all that is contained herein is based upon three decades of combined military, law enforcement, and executive protection training and experience. I suppose you could say that I have worked my whole life amassing that which will be outlined herein.

As an added bonus, the last half of this book includes the original PFT manuscript in a Second Edition format. This endeavor gave me the opportunity go back and polish the first book, something many authors would like to do but cannot due to time and cost issues.

*Note: if you are reading this book and your sword is not within reach, put it down, retrieve your sword and continue.

?

Team Manual

Introduction

If you were fortunate enough to go to a good school or if you have educated yourself, you are likely aware of the famous American fighting force, "Rogers' Rangers." During the French and Indian War (Seven Years War in Europe) Robert Rogers formed a band of fighting men that used, then unconventional, tactics to address the threat posed by the French and their wild Indian allies in the American Colonies.

Rogers essentially learned to fight the Indians at their own game and became so adept at it that he started to beat them at that game. Rogers' troops were well-trained, hard-fighting men and they set the standard for American fighters and U.S. Army Rangers to this day.

The Rangers wrote a set of guidelines and I thought this would be an excellent way to begin this book. While some of the specifics are antiquated due to the advancement of time, the concept behind the "Checklist" and the "Rules" is timeless.

While many of these "Rules" may not apply to your situation. You will be well served to read and understand them. Robert Rogers set the bar high for American fighting men and it is certainly an example worth emulating.

*Note: Robert Rogers did indeed side with Great Britain during the American Revolution. He picked the losing side and never recovered the fame he earned early on in his life. Nonetheless, that fact does not diminish what he accomplished with the formation of his Rangers.

"Ranger Checklist"

1. Don't forget nothing. (*Or, remember everything)

2. Have your musket clean as a whistle, hatchet scoured, sixty rounds powder and ball, and be ready to march at a minute's warning.

3. When you're on the march, act the way you would if you was sneaking up on a deer. See the enemy first.

4. Tell the truth about what you see and do. There is an army depending on us for correct information. You can lie all you please when you tell other folks about the Rangers, but don't never lie to a Ranger or officer.

5. Don't never take a chance you don't have to.

6. When we're on the march we march single file, far enough apart so one shot can't go through two men.

7. If we strike swamps, or soft ground, we spread out abreast, so it's hard to track us.

8. When we march, we keep moving 'til dark, so as to give the enemy the least possible chance at us.

9. When we camp, half the party stays awake while the other half sleeps.

10. If we take prisoners, we keep 'em separate 'til we have had time to examine them, so they can't cook up a story between 'em.

11. Don't ever march home the same way. Take a different route so you won't be ambushed.

12. No matter whether we travel in big parties or little ones, each party has to keep a scout 20 yards ahead, twenty yards on each flank and twenty yards in the rear, so the main body can't be surprised and wiped out.

13. Every night you'll be told where to meet if surrounded by a superior force.

14. Don't sit down to eat without posting sentries.

15. Don't sleep beyond dawn. Dawn's when the French and Indians attack.

16. Don't cross a river by a regular ford.

17. If somebody's trailing you, make a circle, come back onto your own tracks, and ambush the folks that aim to ambush you.

18. Don't stand up when the enemy's coming against you. Kneel down. Hide behind a tree.

19. Let the enemy come 'till he's almost close enough to touch. Then let him have it and jump out and finish him up with your hatchet.

20. Don't use your musket if you can kill 'em with your hatchet. (1)

Robert Rogers "Rules of Ranging"

(some repetition with the 'Checklist')

1. All Rangers are subject to the rules of war.

2. In a small group, march in single file with enough space between so that one shot can't pass through one man and kill a second.

3. Marching over soft ground should be done abreast, making tracking difficult. At night, keep half your force awake while half sleeps.

4. Before reaching your destination, send one or two men forward to scout the area and avoid traps.

5. If prisoners are taken, keep them separate and question them individually.

6. Marching in groups of three or four hundred should be done in three separate columns, within support distance, with a point and rear guard.

7. When attacked, fall or squat down to receive fire and rise to deliver. Keep your flanks as strong as the enemy's flanking force, and if retreat is necessary, maintain the retreat fire drill.

8. When chasing an enemy, keep your flanks strong, and prevent them from gaining high ground where they could turn and fight.

9. When retreating, the rank facing the enemy must fire and retreat through the second rank, thus causing the enemy to advance into constant fire.

10. If the enemy is far superior, the whole squad must disperse and meet again at a designated location. This scatters the pursuit and allows for organized resistance.

11. If attacked from the rear, the ranks reverse order, so the rear rank now becomes the front. If attacked from the flank, the opposite flank now serves as the rear rank.

12. If a rally is used after a retreat, make it on the high ground to slow the enemy advance.

13. When laying in ambuscade, wait for the enemy to get close enough that your fire will be doubly frightening, and after firing, the enemy can be rushed with hatchets.

14. At a campsite, the sentries should be posted at a distance to protect the camp without revealing its location. Each sentry will consist of 6 men with two constantly awake at a time.

15. The entire detachment should be awake before dawn each morning as this is the usual time of enemy attack.

16. Upon discovering a superior enemy in the morning, you should wait until dark to attack, thus hiding your lack of numbers and using the night to aid your retreat.

17. Before leaving a camp, send out small parties to see if you have been observed during the night.

18. When stopping for water, place proper guards around the spot making sure the

pathway you used is covered to avoid surprise from a following party.

19. Avoid using regular river fords as these are often watched by the enemy.

20. Avoid passing lakes too close to the edge, as the enemy could trap you against the water's edge.

21. If an enemy is following your rear, circle back and attack him along the same path.

22. When returning from a scout, use a different path as the enemy may have seen you leave and will wait for your return to attack when you're tired.

23. When following an enemy force, try not to use their path, but rather plan to cut them off and ambush them at a narrow place or when they least expect it.

24. When traveling by water, leave at night to avoid detection.

25. In rowing in a chain of boats, the one in front should keep contact with the one directly astern of it. This way they can help each other and the boats will not become lost in the night.

26. One man in each boat will be assigned to watch the shore for fires or movement.

27. If you are preparing an ambuscade near a river or lake, leave a force on the opposite side of the water so the enemy's flight will lead them into your detachment.

28. When locating an enemy party of undetermined strength, send out a small scouting party to watch them. It may take all day to decide on your attack or withdrawal, so signs and countersigns should be established to determine your friends in the dark.

29. If you are attacked in rough or flat ground, it is best to scatter as if in rout. At a pre-picked place you can turn, allowing the enemy to close. Fire closely, then counterattack with hatchets. Flankers could then attack the enemy and rout him in return. (2)

During the original text "Patriot Fire Team: Preserving the Republic Four Men at a Time" we took the time to establish the "why" part of the Team. We considered in detail the historical precedent of American patriots, militias, and the training bands that were used to forge the greatest nation in the history of the world.

This "Team Manual" is presented to answer the "how" questions. If you have not taken the time to read the first book, now is a good time to do so. Guns and gear are only a part of the equation. A man of means can go out and purchase a Lamborghini, but without an understanding of what he has and the purpose behind the machine, it is simply an expensive toy. This manual is not about toy collecting, it is about the Tools of Liberty.

Sources

(1)   http://www.rjsmith.com/rogers.html

(2)   http://wesclark.com/jw/rogers_r.html

Author's Note and Challenge

In this book you will encounter this symbol [?] periodically. When you see the question mark in a box, I want you to either write down a question to which you are seeking an answer, or write something you learned by studying the manual. Yes, write in your book and take notes for yourself.

[?]

Team Manual

Chapter 1   Dressing for the Part

Tens of thousands of American gun owners have gone online or to stores and purchased "tactical" clothing and gear. Of those thousands, the vast majority have done little but play dress up in the mirror or perhaps gone to the square range all dressed up.

The primary purpose of this chapter is to address the practical and realistic choices for personal clothing, to include footwear. Yes, you can make due with blue jeans and T-shirts, but take it from someone who had to live with two sets of cammies and two pairs of boots for six months, quality clothing makes a difference.

Footwear

Let us begin from the ground up. If your feet are tired, sore, and aching, you will be of little use to yourself and your team. We touched on this in the first book and I am going to go further in detail now.

When it comes to clothing, boots, and gear you need to remember the following words, "Berry Compliant." The Berry Amendment (USC, Title 10, Section 2533a), requires the Department of Defense to give preference in procurement to domestically produced, manufactured, or home-grown products, most notably food, clothing, fabrics, and specialty metals.

What does the Berry Amendment mean to you? It means that it is good enough to be issued to the U.S. Military. If it is good enough to be issued to the U.S. Army or Marine Corps, it should serve you well.

The current "tactical" gear market is flooded with cheap Chinese crap (yes, you can find quality gear made in China, but it is not always easy to come by). Gear that looks "tactical" but is essentially a cheap knock-off of the real thing is fine if all you are doing is playing dress up. For our purposes, we are looking for gear that will stand up to real field use and stress.

Cheap Chinese boots all seem to have the same flaw; the soles fall off. Not immediately mind you, but the makers glue the soles to the boots and after being exposed to the weather; hot, cold, wet, etc. the adhesive gives way and the soles come away from the boots. That is bad news in the field.

I was at a training course once and witnessed a student literally walk right out of the sole of his boot in the mud. The boots were brand new. He had purchased them right before attending the class. This poor guy had to duct-tape the sole of his boot back on and finish the day. Fortunately for the man in question, he was able to go to the store that night and buy new boots. If you are out in the field, far away from civilization, and that happens your life just got very interesting to say the least.

Step number one is to find a quality pair of boots. Step number two, find a second pair of good boots. When it comes to field boots there are two schools of thought. Some people love Goretex® or similar water-resistant boots, some curse them. Water-resistant boots are good for keeping out the morning dew, puddle water and light rain. Once submerged completely they tend to hold the water in and take a long time to dry.

If you plan to be in and out of ankle, knee, chest deep water, a better choice of boots will be ones that have vents to allow the water to run out and material that is quick drying. We used to simply call these "jungle boots".

Of course, boots with open vents suck in the desert as they allow fine, powdery sand to get in. During the first Gulf War, when my battalion deployed directly from the Okinawa jungles to the Kuwaiti desert, most all of us were wearing Vietnam era jungle boots. The new suede leather desert boots did not get to us until AFTER the fighting was over. We used to melt our plastic MRE spoons into the vents on our jungle boots to keep the sand out.

If you anticipate that you will be constantly in water, especially cold water, some type of rubber boot should be considered. In dry, powdery snow you can get away with Goretex boots, not so in half-melted slushy snow and cold wet mud.

The best advice I can offer for boots is to purchase some type of water-resistant boots and an additional set of quick drying, lightweight boots. You can rotate them for the weather and the environment as needed. To get the best wear from your boots you should rotate them on a regular basis. Invest in quality socks and you will never regret it. Yes, it is tempting to walk into your local discount store and buy a six pack of socks for six bucks, but you get what you pay for. As a matter of fact, you will not likely find decent boot socks at a discount store.

Wool is the go to material for quality boot socks. Yes, there are blends as well, but thick, cushioned wool socks are the standard. Wool socks wick away moisture from your feet and add the all-important cushion between the boot and the foot. When I say "wool sock", I am not talking about super-thick arctic socks, merely wool construction.

Innumerable outdoor clothing makers have quality socks. Expect to pay ten to twenty dollars a pair. Yes, that is pricey for regular socks, but not quality boot socks. If your feet are sore and blistered, you are going to be hating life in the field. You have enough to worry about without fretting over sore feet. And, yes, you wear wool socks in hot weather too.

Woolrich, Vermont, Blackhawk, and Land's End are all good places to start looking for quality boot socks. REI (Recreation Equipment Inc.) is kind of a hippie, granola-eater store but they sell high quality outdoor gear, including boots and socks.

Clothing

As for shirts and pants, again, we must consider quality and durability. Blue jeans and T-shirts will get you by, but they are not designed for serious outdoor/field use. Mobility and comfort are the primary concerns after durability. Military/tactical pants have looser tolerance in the crotchal region to allow the user to sit, kneel, and squat without the binding of normal pants. You should also consider that you may be climbing into, or over, vehicles and obstacles or crawling under them.

Pockets are a big consideration. This is where normal blue jeans fail the test. Blue jean pockets are good for a wallet, some change, maybe a small pocket knife, but that's about it. In the field you will be shoving a plethora of objects into various pockets either for normal carry or hasty storage. Most tactical pants have a slot/pocket in the knee area to allow a foam knee pad to be added. Historically the "knee pads" shipped with the pants are little more than cheap "mouse pads."

The most comfortable, highest quality knee pad insert I have ever found comes from a company called "Alta." I found the Alta "Shockguard" knee pads at a police supply store and fell in love with them. They are worth every penny of the twenty-five bucks I paid. Alta also makes external/hard shell knee pads as well.

I have discussed belts adnauseum in regard to concealed carry. A durable nylon belt that is 1.5 to 1.75 inches wide should be high on your priority list. There are too many companies making quality field belts to name here. The Wilderness Tactical makes the belt I wear most every day. Original S.O.E. Gear has a reputation for quality belts as well. As with quality socks, you will not regret purchasing a strong, durable belt.

As for undergarments, I will leave you only with this advice. Cotton drawers hold in moisture during hot weather, not a good combination. Under Armor and similar designs cost more but offer more comfort. Most troops in the jungle or desert will forego drawers all together.

T-shirts, on the other hand, are important to keep your uniform blouse or tactical shirt from chafing and rubbing you raw. Always pack one or two more than you think you will need. A fresh, dry T-shirt in the field can make you feel like a new man.

Remember to add a soft cover (hat) to the list. Ball caps of various styles will work. Stay away from mesh hats. The hat is supposed to protect your head from the rays of the sun. A cloth "boonie" or "jungle" hat with a wraparound brim is a great addition to the kit, particularly if you anticipate lying in the prone position (behind a scoped rifle) for an extended period of time.

Foul Weather Gear

In the heat you need to remove layers, stay in the shade and drink a lot of water (do not forget sunscreen). For the other weather extremes; wind, wet, cold, and the dreaded cold, wet and windy, you need to be prepared. The elements can make you miserable, sick, and even kill you if you are not prepared.

The reason this section is so important is that modern man has become so comfortable that have lost the basic survival skills. I have lost count of the times I've watched twenty-something men run from their car to a business in sub-freezing temperatures without so much as a jacket. We have become conditioned to move from warm dry house to warm dry car to warm dry business without ever considering what would happen if the warm dry car broke down or was involved in a crash.

Recently, people in Atlanta, Georgia were stranded by a freak snow storm. Motorists trapped on the road by the weather were freezing, as they did not have the basic essential clothing for winter weather.

Layering is the key to all things foul weather related. Beginning from the inside out, you will have your normal field clothing. Atop your clothes you can add a rain jacket shell and rain pants or you can simply don a military grade poncho. Ponchos are utilitarian in nature but do not lend themselves well to actual fighting or serious field work.

Fleece jackets in various weights and thickness can be worn alone for cold, or under the rain jacket for cold and wet. Speaking of fleece, you have no reason not to purchase a fleece watch cap/hat. They store easily in your jacket pocket and are priceless when the mercury drops.

Just as importantly, you can wear a fleece watch cap under a ballistic helmet, unlike the old thick wool hats we used to be issued. Don't get me wrong, a wool knit cap will keep your noggin warm, but we used to have to remove them to secure our Kevlar helmets.

Your jackets, fleece and rain, should have ample room for arm movement. If they fit too tightly they will negatively affect circulation to your arms. That is naturally a bad thing. Your foul weather clothing should fit in a way that allows you to continue your mission unhindered. If you cannot climb in and out of a truck because your rain suit is binding, that is a clue.

If your base clothing is wet, it is best to remove it before donning your over layers. Of course, the mission will dictate whether this is practical. Nothing makes a man more miserable in the field than to be wet and cold. Hypothermia is a genuine concern and must be fought like an enemy.

Shemagh

Back during the Vietnam and during the Cold War eras, every new G.I. Med Kit came with a "military cravat, triangular bandage, O.D. green". These green pieces of cloth were tough muslin fabric and useful for many applications. Naturally, the stated purpose for the O.D. cravat was to make a sling or bandage. We would wear them as head scarves under our Kevlar helmets. Wearing a cravat on your head all by itself was strictly frowned upon, but that did not stop us from occasionally trying to get away with it in the field when we played the aggressor role or did nocturnal patrolling.

The shemagh of today is what the O.D. cravat was twenty years ago, only better. The modern shemagh is made of a more absorbent and breathable material. They are thicker than the cravats and a bit larger. Like its predecessor, the military shemagh can be used as a face or head scarf, an arm sling or expedient tourniquet, a sweat wiping cloth or it can be spread out on the ground to catch any small parts during a field cleaning of your weapons.

Snipers and designated marksman can drape a shemagh over their heads and rifle scope to break up their silhouette and minimize the signature. A shemagh can be laid out on the ground under the muzzle of a rifle to prevent the dust signature when taking a prone shot.

The modern military shemagh is an invaluable piece of gear that is well worth the price. It is highly recommended that you buy at least one, if not two, to keep in your pack.

Sources

http://uspatriottactical.com/berry-compliant-boots-shoes/⬜

Team Manual

Chapter 2   Deuce Gear

Given the origins of the Fire Team, I thought it appropriate to title this chapter "Deuce Gear". Back in the old Corps, (damn, I can get away with saying that now) when a young troop checked in to a new unit one of their first stops was "Supply" (the supply depot) to draw their individual field gear.

Unlike their personal uniforms, boots, socks, etc. field gear generally was the property of the unit, not the individual Marine. Each time a man would check in with a new unit they would draw the "Individual Field Gear" from the list designated for that specific unit based upon that unit's primary mission.

For instance, some infantry units were designated as "cold weather", some as "jungle warfare", some as "boat teams", etc. It would be a waste of time and resources to issue the 25th Marines with mosquito nets and swim fins if their primary mission is "Cold Weather and Mountain Warfare."

However, regardless of their mission, most every trooper was indeed issued a basic set of field gear. This list would include a Kevlar helmet, body armor, load-bearing gear, a gas mask, bayonet or fighting knife, rain poncho, etc. The official form used as a receipt for this gear was called NAVMC Form 782. From that title, Marines started to refer to their field gear as "782 gear" or simply "Deuce gear" for short.

Deuce gear is all of the extra "stuff" that you may need to accomplish the mission. During this chapter we are going to consider, in detail, mission critical gear and accessories. We will also discuss what is practical for your particular neck of the woods. As in the previous example, it makes little sense for a team in Savannah, Georgia to invest money in snow parkas and sub-zero boots.

Load-Bear Equipment

Back in the old days we made use of web belts, harnesses and suspenders to carry all of the miscellaneous gear. Along came the Global War on Terror and almost overnight American gear makers began producing a plethora of load-bearing equipment options.

Whether you call it Modular Lightweight Load-carrying Equipment (MOLLE), STRIKE, PALS, webbing based gear has largely replaced the old ALICE (All-Purpose Light-Weight Individual Carrying Equipment).

MOLLE gear has the benefit of being extremely easy to modify and adjust for the mission and the individual. For better than a decade, that system has been used with great success by troops overseas. MOLLE is simply a series of straps sewn to the outside of a carrier. Pouches and holders of various designs are affixed to the carrier by weaving the straps in and out. Think about the construction paper placemats and art projects you did in elementary school.

You will find MOLLE webbing on vests, plate carriers, body armor, backpacks, and other platforms. The only downside might be that with so many options to choose from, it can be difficult for the beginner to know what is practical and what is superfluous. Let's start with some basics that everyone will need, regardless of mission or area of operation (AO).

If you are equipped with a firearm, you will need to have some way to carry spare/extra ammunition for that gun. Bare minimum for magazine fed rifles is three (3) magazines. If a handgun is a secondary gun, not the primary, you will need a minimum of two (2) extra magazines in addition to the one in the pistol.

Shotgun ammunition can be carried in loops or pouches, depending on your desire. Loops are fast and convenient but expose ammunition to the outside elements. A medium to large pouch with a cover that can be secured can get you by in a pinch. Most dedicated shotgun guys will use a combination of both. Loops for fast reloads, pouches to carry bulk ammunition.

When it comes to rifle magazines, many companies offer vests and carriers with mag pouches built in to the unit. What is the best choice? The answer is quite simple; it is up to the user. Just like Coke® and Pepsi®, some folks swear by one style and other the opposite. The benefit of individual MOLLE pouches is that you can alter your load. How often will you want to do that? That is a question that only you can answer.

As far as setup is concerned, your support hand will be doing the majority of reaching and grabbing for magazines. However, it is a good idea from a tactical standpoint to be able to reach your spare ammo with either hand. Generally speaking, reloads come faster from the support side of the body. This goes for rifles or pistols. Remember, keep it simple. Wherever you choose to stage your spare ammo, be consistent. In the middle of a fight you do not want to be playing the "Where is my ammo?" game.

That brings me to a valid point. Once you set up your gear, you need to get out to the field and actually use it. What might have seemed like a great idea in your bedroom may be a disaster in the field. Can you reach your magazines while standing, kneeling, prone, on your back, in a vehicle? These are important questions and you might not realize the answers until you get out and train.

Just as important, be consistent. After you have set up your gear the way you like it, leave it alone! You should be able to reach your gear without having to wonder where it is or search for it. If you keep a folding knife in your left pocket, keep it there all the time. Resist the urge to move it around from pocket to pocket. Ditto times ten for pistols.

Medical pouches (blow out kits) should always be in the same place, not just on you, but on the entire team. Your med kit is there to save your life. Do not make it difficult for your team members because you moved it somewhere that is hard to find.

Blow out kits should be in a position where you can reach them with either hand, from any position. This normally means up front on your LBE. Back on the old days we used to fall into stupid "institutionalized" traps. The unit commander might have thought that the first aid kit looked the most "uniform" centered on top of the trooper's "ass pack". Try reaching your med kit when it is located right over your ass while you are wearing body armor. I dare you.

Keeping with the "Beans, Bullets, and Band Aids" mantra, we have talked about ammunition and med kits. Brothers (and sisters) you are going to need water. GI canteens made of newer polymer are a good place to start and you will need pouches to carry them. Getting a drink is not tactically critical in a fight, but you should be able to reach your water without taking off your gear.

There are multiple types and styles of water bladders that can be carried in the middle of your back. This is a valid idea as the weight of the water (water is heavy) is displaced and easier to carry. Water bladders come with a drinking hose that you can set up for easy access. The downside of water bladders is that you normally have to take off your gear to refill them. So, I suppose you can say it is a tradeoff.

On the subject of canteens and water bladders, take my advice and purchase those made with the new antimicrobial polymer. This will greatly reduce the funk that grows in them that can make you sick. DO NOT put sugary liquid in your canteens and water bladders (or do, and then pay the price later). Foreign made, cheap Chinese water bladders seem like a bargain until they leak and the seals fail in the field. In the field WATER is LIFE. (No, I am not giving you my water because you decided to be a cheap ass and buy a junk bladder at a gun show)

*Bonus Material: The Gear Enabler

In every unit there is a guy who thinks that he can just "borrow" this or that when they get to the field. This person is generally lazy and or undisciplined. They left their rain poncho at home or they forgot to fill their canteens. Perhaps they knew their flashlight batteries were dying but thought, "I will just borrow a light if I need it."

When this person is cold, wet, or thirsty they will look to other members of the team to "borrow" what they should have brought, what everyone else took the time to bring. "But Paul, you said team members should support each other." Yes, I did say that. I am not telling you to let someone freeze to death or die of dehydration.

If you loan out your poncho so that guy can stand watch in the rain or you give them your spare flashlight batteries the lesson they will learn is this: no sweat, someone will just loan me what I forgot. Conversely, if the subject gets soaked to the bone standing in the rain they will never forget their poncho again. It is the 'teach a man to fish' or give a man a fish concept.

You are not doing your alcoholic brother-in-law any favors by giving him 20 bucks "just one last time" every time he asks for it. Have the courage to say "no" and eventually he will fix himself.

Hopefully you will have a team of disciplined, motivated people and this will not be the case. Long story short, do not be the "gear enabler."

*Even More Bonus Material

Pack Your Bag: Minimum Gear List

Like the Minute Man of 1775, you should have a bag staged that you can grab and go. What follows is a piece originally published for the SOTG Grad Program in the Tactical Tutor newsletter.

It is easy to get overwhelmed by all of the choices of gear that are out there. It is also just as easy to get buried under a ton of gear that seemed like a good idea when you saw the ad but now you have a hundred pounds of gear and naturally cannot carry it all.

With a few exceptions, the Go Bag list that follows is very similar to what I carried as a United State Marine Infantryman. If you have a limited budget or are not all that interested in gear, what follows is enough to get you by in a crisis.

A couple of years ago, my friend James Yeager moved from semi-famous to famous with his much discussed and controversial "Pack your bags" YouTube video. I am not here to discuss the pros and cons of the video or the aftermath, but the concept behind the video that was eclipsed by the media firestorm that transpired.

The terms "Go Bag" or "Bug Out Bag" have been all the rage for at least five years, perhaps longer. Essentially the idea is to have a backpack or similar container packed and pre-staged with gear for a crisis or "bug out" situation.

"Rational" or "reasonable" people in the gun culture have met this idea with disdain and criticism. Even seasoned gun people have accused Bug Out Bag proponents of living in a paranoid fantasy world. "Do you really think you can survive in the woods for any length of time?" The reasonable folks will say. Or, they will counter with, "Why would you purposely leave your house when that is where you will be safest?"

There is some logic in these counter-points. During many storms or emergencies, sheltering in your home may be the best answer. Also, for someone who has never actually lived in the field or resorted to living off the land, bugging out to the woods is a rather impractical plan.

Practical Reality

There are two prime reasons, at least for the purposes of our discussion, to have a Go Bag packed. First, there is an unavoidable reason to leave the shelter of your home; hurricane, wildfire, earthquake, plague, etc. The second, and more likely scenario, is the need and/or desire to go to the aid of another. Your home might be intact, but the home or community of your friends, family, neighbors has been damaged, destroyed, or threatened with destruction.

A perfect example of such a situation are the most recent tornado touchdowns all over the South and Midwest. From a more historic standpoint, we had the aftermath of Hurricane Katrina, or Ike, Andrew, Hugo, etc.

If the time comes to jump into a truck to go and provide aid, comfort, and relief to your neighbors, packing your bag for the trip is not what you are going to want to be doing. You will pack in a hurry, with other things on your mind, and will neglect/forget something important.

Take the time, when all is calm, to consider what you need in your pack and organize it appropriately. This is a skill I learned long ago as a young US Marine Corps infantryman.

I understand that we have covered this topic in various forms before. My aim for this section is to encourage you to move from the notional, or good intention, stage to the physical reality stage. I don't want you to just agree with me on the concept of the Go Bag and why to have one, I want you to actually take the time to assemble one. Then I want you to have it at the ready.

Before this year is out, I fear most of you will indeed need to grab that bag and act. If you are serious about this undertaking, please continue with the application below. I am going to give you a very specific gear list. You, as a free man or woman, can make substitutions as you see fit.

The Bag

Some folks have offered that prior to choosing a bag, you should first figure out exactly what it is you plan to carry. After that decision is made, then you will shop for a bag that is the correct size to tote all of your "stuff". That is valid advice to be certain. I am about to make your life very simple: ALICE pack, Medium.

*Caution: ALICE packs have removable / replaceable shoulder straps. Some companies will sell you a low cost pack because it has no shoulder straps.

Regarding the aluminum ALICE pack frame, unless you plan to hump long distances you don't really need one. Yes, they are important for humping/hiking. If you have the cash go ahead and buy one.

Poncho

Rain suits are nice, but you cannot drape a rain suit over your gear to shelter it from foul weather or string it up to make a shelter/shade from the scorching sun. You should absolutely invest in a military-grade rain poncho. Inexpensive plastic ponchos will shred and come apart during hard use or in heavy wind. As for camouflage pattern, IDGAF, suit yourself. Nylon/Ripstop ponchos are lighter than the older rubberized versions. The rubberized versions tend to be tougher and take more abuse. Prices range from $20 to $50 online.

Poncho Liner

A poncho liner is an essential piece of field gear. Buy one and store it in your pack. Yes, sleeping bags can be more comfortable and keep you warmer; however, the poncho liner is worth its weight in gold. Trust me. Again, as for camo pattern, IDGAF, do as you like. Online prices from Amazon range from $20 to $50 depending on whether or not it is new or used.

Undergarments

When you grab your Go Bag and boogie you will very likely already be dressed. You can survive with the clothes on your back. But...you will soon be funky and miserable if you do not have a change of undergarments. T-shirts, underwear, and socks are, specifically, that of which I speak. Pack a few extra cotton T-shirts in your pack. Not your favorite cool guy shirts, but the ones in your dresser that you never wear. You won't miss them in the bottom of the Go Bag. I would put a minimum of (3) T-shirts in my Go Bag.

Men, you can go without underwear, but keep in mind, they shield your pants from your ass. Cotton underdrawers work, but in the summer they will hold in the moisture and you'll end up with crotch rot. Bad juju!

Under Armor or similar breathable under shorts are more expensive, but they will save your nuts from the funk. They are your balls, do what you will. Ladies, I'm only a vagina enthusiast not a woman, so treat yours accordingly.

You will never regret a fresh, dry, clean pair of socks. Wet, dirty, funky socks are going to chap your feet. Miserable feet equal bad day, bad week, etc. Even if you only have one pair of boots, change your socks every day. Rinse out the funky ones, repeat as necessary. Put all of your clean/fresh undergarments into a waterproof bag of some sort. One-gallon ZipLock bags are the foshizzle for such tasks. That way, even if you pack gets soaked by rain in the back of a truck you will still have dry undergarments, GOLD in the field.

Some type of Shemagh or OD green cravat is also highly recommended. The nod goes to the modern Shemagh. Tell your jack ass neighbor to suck it when he asks if you think you're "some kinda Arab with that rag on your head?" Fuck him, he'll wish he had one someday. OD green cravat is $1 on Amazon. Shemagh will set you back $10 to $20. The Shemagh is a better piece of kit.

Gloves

Again, I am going to make it easy for you. Buy whichever pair of Mechanix gloves strikes your fancy. Average cost $10 to $20 depending on how fancy you want to get. *Beware of ordering gloves online. The Chinese slaves that made them don't always adhere to Yankee size charts.

Do yourself a favor and try them on at the auto parts store. These are safe to purchase online if you know what size to get. If you are traveling to an area struck by a tornado or hurricane there is going to be debris everywhere. You do not want to be moving that crap barehanded. Cut your hands in the field and there you are again in that bad day, bad week, bad juju situation. I am a fan of having one primary and a secondary pair of gloves. Two is one, one is none is the mantra.

One final thought on gloves, regardless of the brand or design you purchase, for the love of all that is Holy, stop cutting off the fingers. Do not tell me you cannot shoot accurately with gloves on, that is horseshit. I shot every single round while wearing gloves when I attended a sniper school several years ago.

The gloves are supposed to protect your very important and critical digits. Cutting the fingers off defeats the purpose. Stop it! If you having a difficult time operating your gear with your gloves on a) spend more time practicing while wearing gloves b) get new gloves that fit/feel better.

Miscellaneous Good Stuff

Remember the one gallon Ziplock bags? Grab one of the bags and put the following items into it.

One (1) 3ft mini-roll of duct tape, color choice is yours.

One (1) 50 ft. wrap of 550 cord (Purple with pink highlights works best in the field. I'm kidding buy whatever color you like.)

Two (2) Large, heavy duty safety pins (Vets understand)

One (1) Sharpie type marker (just trust me)

One (1) Disposable cigarette lighter

*Optional Items

One (1) Small bottle of Iodine Tablets for emergency water purification (2 tabs per quart of water/canteen)

One (1) Mylar "space" blanket, give to others in an emergency and wrap trauma victims to prevent hypothermia

Food and Water

The Dollar Store, Family Dollar, whatever, sell extra-large (50 oz) bottles of drinking water from less than a buck. Buy one, put it in the pack and forget about it. Purchase a Military quality MRE (not that knock-off shit) and stick it in the pack.

MRE's have a ton of calories and are specifically made to provide essential vitamins, minerals, etc. Choose whatever meal floats your boat. This MRE/Water combo will get you by for a day in a pinch until you can resupply. Remember the mantra "Never get in/on a vehicle without water and food."⏺

Team Manual

Chapter 3

The Most Important Element: You

Whether we are discussing a short-term event like a personal defense scenario, one that begins and ends in moments, a short crisis that lasts a couple of days or a prolonged emergency scenario that goes on for weeks like we saw after Hurricane Katrina, the most important element is you. Yes, your mind and body.

Guns, gear, survival supplies, etc. are all well and good, but without a healthy mind and body to employ them, they are all just "stuff". You cannot buy expensive enough gear to make up for an unhealthy body, a clouded mind, or a lack of knowledge and training. Buying gear is the easy part, and sadly, it is the part that most people focus all of their effort upon.

We all have that friend that likes to brag about their latest purchase. They bought a rail system for their rifle, or a scope or a laser or a new stock, but they have not spent one dollar on training. There are guys that have a $2500 custom M1911 pistol in a $100 holster but cannot make it up a flight of stairs without taking a break.

Before you get on your high horse and tell me about physical infirmity, climb back down. (Most gear hoarders couldn't get on the back of a horse anyway) I am not discussing genuine physical infirmity or handicap. I've been on the training range with men who were missing limbs, legs and arms, and have been humbled by their "can do" spirit. If a man or woman with a prosthetic arm or two bionic legs can get their ass to the range for a training course, what the hell is your excuse?

No, I do not expect every patriot to be an athlete or qualify for Force Recon, but you should be able to make it to lunch time without taking a nap. Our nation is the greatest excuse making culture in the world and we have grown soft and weak. The sad truth is that it is a good thing there are two oceans bordering this country or the Russians would walk over and bitch slap this nation and the pussies and weaklings in charge.

Harden the Fuck Up: Mind

In other words, it is time for you to harden the fuck up. We all harden up in our own ways. A 55-year-old man can be a hard man. As a matter of fact, sadly, we have men in their fifties and sixties that are far tougher and more manly that those in their twenties and thirties.

The fact that you have this book in your hand tells me that your mind is in the right place. You might not be where you want to be at this moment, but you have the drive. Good, we all start somewhere.

In the first Patriot Fire Team book we laid the groundwork for having a strong, educated mind. We offered numerous books to read and listed patriotic source material. If you somehow missed those recommendations and considerations, you should familiarize yourself with the first PFT book (benevolently offered as a 2nd Edition at the end of this manual). There will be some redundancy here between the two, but the effort will be not to simply rewrite that text into this one.

Exercise your mind, give your brain a workout. Read often. Ebooks and online articles are nice, but nothing quite beats the traditional dead-tree version of a book for mental exercise.

I am assuming that you are long since out of primary school as you read this, but you must understand that the reason why math is so important to a developing mind is because it teaches problem solving skills. Think back to the old days when your teacher assigned "math problems" for you to solve. That was not an accident or a time killing exercise.

Shortchanging our kids when it comes to math and science robs them of the ability to problem solve or at least consider problems with a critical or analytical mind. Our modern schools are substituting feelings for facts and cranking out legions of soft-minded, emotion-driven oxygen thieves. These creatures are easy to control because they base all their decisions upon emotion or feelings, not facts and logic.

Challenge yourself. Read the U.S. Constitution and then read the Federalist Papers. Read John Locke's treatise on Natural Rights, Liberty, and Property Rights. Study the history of the American Revolution, the War of Northern Aggression, and World War I and II. *Warning: Any text book published after 1992 is highly suspect.

Even if you are not a Christian, read the book of Proverbs. It is a relatively short book of the Bible and King Solomon might as well have written those words for you and I today as much as he did for people 2000 years ago. When you do read the Bible, consider mentally substituting the word "rifle" when you encounter the word "sword" as you go. Read Matthew 10:34 and insert the word "rifle".

Harden the Fuck Up: Body

Step Number One: be intellectually honest with yourself. Are you where you want to be physically? If the answer is "yes", keep doing that thing and expand your skill set. Get more training. The greatest firearms trainers in the world are the best students. Paul Howe (US Army Special Forces, Detachment Delta) wrote, "Selection is a never ending process." We like to say, you are beginner once, a student for life.

If that honest answer to the aforementioned question is "no", it is time to set realistic goals for yourself. How far can you run without being forced to stop by cramps or vomiting? Even if the answer is 100 feet, set your goal at 150 feet. Don't like to run? Me neither. Get on a treadmill, set the speed for a fast walk (4 mph). If you can go for 15 minutes without cramping up, set your goal for 20 minutes.

Pushups, planks, sit ups, squats, whatever form of exercise you are comfortable with, do as many/much as you can and set your goal for one more, two more, five more repetition or pounds. You get the drill. Write down your starting point. Set a goal to increase after one week, then two weeks, a month.

By setting goals, and then meeting those goals you are not only improving your overall physical condition, you are disciplining your mind. The two work in close consort with each other. Encourage your fire team. If a team member can do a mere three pushups, encourage them to do four.

Practical Exercises

Remember all that gear you bought? Did you buy a load bearing vest, plate carrier, soft body armor, a backpack, rifle, pistol, drop leg holster, boots, clothes? Put it all on and spend eight hours on the training range. If you have a backpack set aside as your "bug out bag", put it on your back, lace up your boots and go for a walk. How far did you get?

Your gear is not going to carry itself. In the Marine Corps Infantry, I learned the art of "field stripping" gear. We would go through our packs and eliminate any and all unnecessary weight. When you look at a piece of gear I want you to think "Is this worth carrying five miles?" If the answer is "no" it must not be that important. If the answer is "yes" then you need to be in good enough physical shape to lug it around.

No, I don't expect you to take a Fighting Pistol class with a backpack on the entire time, but you need to be able to carry your gear to the place where the fighting is going to take place. Basic load bearing gear, spare ammunition, med kit, knife, water, etc. are all items that you should be able to carry around all day long. If you cannot do that you need to harden the fuck up. Seven full 30 round magazines seem like a prudent idea until you realize that your gear weight is pulling you down. The choice is simple, less gear or more muscle.

If you are carrying firearms as a part of a security mission (protecting your home and property from looters after a storm), you might consider balancing out the ammunition weight with water, med gear, tactical flashlight, and a radio. One or two extra magazines balanced with the aforementioned gear would seem to be more sensible that simply walking around with 10 pounds of ammo on your chest.

More than lifting heavy weights or running for long distances, the most important type of fitness is the ability to be on your feet for extended periods of time. Leg and back strength are key in this equation. We have already discussed the subject of quality boots and socks, now we will focus on the feet and legs.

If you engage in no other form of exercise for your PFT commitment, get your butt outside and walk. No, I don't mean walk to the car, I mean walk for a few miles. Back roads or sidewalks are convenient as they are cleared and paved, but the concrete or asphalt will be tough on your feet and legs. Trail walking is an excellent form of exercise if you can manage it. Don't forget your pack.

⁇

Team Manual

Chapter 4   Weapons

Some "reasonable" folks out there would advise against using the term "weapon" in anything other than a true military text. Those people would try to convince you that only those sanctioned by the government should possess "weapons".

Unlike the peasantry of the majority of the world, a United States Citizen has the unique opportunity and obligation to be the defender of his community and country. Armed with the affirmation of his God-given rights, the US Citizen is obliged to possess weapons, not tools for sport, but weapons with which to preserve the Republic.

This topic of weapons a perfect opportunity to review an excellent quote from John Steinbeck:

The purpose of fighting is to win. There is no possible victory in defense. The sword is more important than the shield, and skill is more important than either. The final weapon is the brain. All else is supplemental.

When the subject of weapons arises, always keep the Steinbeck quote in mind. Too often we look to the object to solve our problems for us.

Many American men behave as if the more money they spend on guns and gear, the more skillful they will become. The weapon merely augments the skill of the user. Ownership of an object does not impart the ability to use said object.

In the original Patriot Fire Team book, we offer our recommendations for arms. The Patriot Arsenal and Patriot Arsenal on a Budget were outlined in detail as well as ammunition selection. (Chapter 7 PFT book)

This chapter is deliberately kept brief. By the time you read this book you have likely already devoted a great deal of your attention the subject of arms. There are innumerable training schools and courses you can attend to improve your firearms skills. This is not just another "gun book". We need more than firearms to preserve the Republic.▨

Chapter 5 Signaling: Lights, Smoke, and Pyro

The difference between a successful fire team and an armed mob is training, planning, and communication. During this part of the Team Manual we are going to focus on communication via signaling.

"Comms" in the military vernacular generally refers to radios, crypto gear, sat-phones, etc. However, communication takes place via many methods and verbal communication is just one way. Sights and sounds are common ways that teams communicate with each other when talking is not practical or possible.

Humans take in somewhere in the neighborhood of eighty-five to ninety percent of all their sensory input through their eyes, depending on which study you source. Understanding that fact, we must be prepared to use visual communication methods with our team.

Hand and arms signals are some of the most common visual communication tools you have at your disposal. You have been using them all of your life and probably never thought about it. The "thumbs up" gesture is universally accepted as "all is well" or "good". Conversely, "thumbs down" is recognized as negative "all is not well" or "bad" signal.

There are numerous hand and arm signals used universally by US military personnel. The Marine Rifle Squad Manual MCWP 3-11.2 has sketches and detailed explanations of all the commonly used military hand and arm signals, to include those used in a landing zone (LZ) to direct in a helicopter. You can purchase the Rifle Squad Manual in paperback or download a PDF version.

Naturally, hand and arm signals are used when the noise of gunfire makes it difficult to hear. We also use hand signals when we are trying to be quiet and talking would give away our position or intentions. Something as simple as wind noise can make verbal communication in the field difficult. Communication or signaling methods need to have redundancy just like any other part of the tactical plan.

Handheld or weapon-mounted lights are naturally used to identify friend from foe in poor lighting conditions. Lights can also be for signaling purposes.

Night Fighting: Understanding Tactical Lights Dynamics

Shane Iversen MSgt US Army SF, Retired

CSAT MTT

0330 local, January 2006, 40 kilometers west of Tal Afar, Iraq a column of four US Army HMMWVs along with ten Iraqi police trucks containing the 90 man Tal Afar SWAT Team moved slowly towards a group of four tents containing a group of insurgents camped along a wadi. SIGINT had confirmed the presence of our target and we were intent on capturing or killing him along with his cohorts.

Since the objective was located in open desert the plan was to assault on line in our vehicles using speed to gain surprise and hopefully keep the bad guys from reaching the wadi nearby. Experience had taught us that we didn't want to get into another gun fight in a wadi if we could help it. Encounters such as that tended to turn into hand grenade fights and nobody wanted that.

As we closed to within 300 meters of the objective we turned on our white lights and launched parachute flares to illuminate the area for our Iraqi counterparts who were not equipped with Night Optical Devices (NODs).

Instantly, the enemy started to make for the wadi and machinegun fire began to come our way. The SWAT truck to my left burst into flames. This was going to be a tough one.

Our trucks came abreast of the enemy PKM position as he was still hammering the soft skin SWAT truck, I ordered a halt. Having pulled my NODs up when we went to white lights during the approach. I exited the front passenger door to engage the enemy gunner. Hitting him with my white light I immediately drew his full attention as he shifted fire back to our vehicle. Bad decision, as Murphy's law had reared his ugly head and the M-240 machinegun I was illuminating for malfunctioned. Always a quick learner, I flipped my NODs down and serviced the bad guy with my M-4 carbine and PAC-2 while the 240 was down.

What was reinforced to me that night was that there is no one tool or solution for fighting at night, as the unexpected always occurs. You have to be thinking and your equipment and tactics have to cover a broad spectrum of possibilities.

HISTORY

The last 15 years have been marked by a dramatic increase in tactical tools and technology. One of the categories where that is most evident is tactical lights. In 2002 we were issued our first purpose-built gun light; a Surefire Millennium series model. Recalling the first time I used it at night in Afghanistan, it was utterly amazing how powerful the light was when I illuminated a pile of rocks about 100 meters out from the HMMWV turret I was manning.

Back then my team and I were in awe of the SureFire's compact size; a mere 6 inches long and lighter than a pound. We had come a long way from taping lights to our guns for night raids and ambushes. That model light had an incandescent bulb and it ran on three BA123 lithium batteries. The light got hot enough to melt the plastic Butler Creek scope cover I retrofitted to prevent a "White Light ND" (negligent discharge/activation of light). Not only did that light work, but it worked exceedingly well and never failed.

Looking back now, it seems like the Stone Age and I remember thinking, "Man, good things are happening. We have night vision, lasers and purpose built gun lights. We own the night and all of our problems are solved!" Nowadays, everything about that particular gun light is antiquated and I have come to realize that we had just began to scratch the surface of fighting in the dark.

Today's state-of-the-art tactical lights use LED bulbs, which can project vastly higher lumens of white light and, with a twist of a bezel ring, turn the unit into an infrared flood light. All this using just a single BA123 Lithium or even double AA batteries that will run for weeks. All of those features now come in a two to three-inch aluminum or polymer cases weighing only a few ounces.

You can spend a ton of time and money on lights. I have to admit; all the advances do sometimes get me to salivating. However, at heart I am a simple creature. It is very hard to get me to buy new equipment when I still have very serviceable and capable equipment on hand, especially if it has proven reliable and effective. I have been issued more Surefire lights than any other brand over the years. I consistently found their products to be reliable and high quality. Consequently, I developed a great deal trust for the brand based on that experience set.

Surefire supports their line of tactical lights with multiple accessories that can enhance, upgrade, and reconfigure any existing light you may possess to fit just about any mission or application of which you can think. With a little research and ingenuity, you can keep that old light up to date with new technology. If you have been using Surefire products, they may very well offer upgrade components to bring your light up to the latest technology specs for much less than a new light system might cost.

I currently run an Inforce weapon mounted light and a Fenix hand held. Through my experience, both lights have been great and I have given them some hard use to develop a good trust and frame of reference for performance. They are doing very well on both counts.

TACTICAL CONSIDERATIONS:

First, let me offer you this general guideline to govern your choice; higher lumens are better. Yes, you can make an argument that too much light can blind you in a house or enclosed space if it reflects off a light colored surface. As far as I am concerned, I'll take that calculated chance when I weigh the gains I get from being able to truly disrupt an opponent's OODA Loop* at close range by dazing him with a 1000 Lumen light and regain the initiative in a fight. A second but critical point that we need to discuss is how Lumen power aids in target discrimination, especially when you are outside.

I think we can all agree that being aware of a threat is a critical performance point in gun fighting. Situational Awareness (SA) is a basic and well understood skill set. One of the primary tools of gaining SA is through our ability to see. Hence the evolution of the gun light and tactical hand held lights. Being able to discriminate that a form we have identified with our naked eye in low light is a difficult task, especially if that form is attempting to conceal a weapon. The ability to illuminate a threat and discriminate whether we actually need to engage or not is based on our ability to see details. This is where Lumen power aids us the most.

Using a general rule that we can actually identify a weapon in low light at about 15 yards we can start to see that adding more light to the problem will help us in discriminating friend from foe by allowing us to see greater detail from further away. If you understand that we want to expand our reaction time while reducing our opponent's ability to act, then it stands to reason that being able to discern more details of an identified form from a greater distance will allow us more time to make a decision to shoot or not to shoot.

Using a powerful light will also give us other choices, such as; take cover, create more distance, or break contact from the situation. I like to look at it as this; distance = time, time = options, options = initiative. Bottom line; the benefits you get from higher lumens far outweigh the few disadvantages. Always bet with the greater advantage ratio.

TECHNICAL CONSIDERATIONS:

Now, since we have discussed some of the tactical considerations, let's look at some technical considerations that can help us decide on what light to run and how they can aid us in our tactics. A person can get caught up in all of the specs of batteries and their run times as well as whatever space age circuitry one flashlight or another has, but for me the simpler the better.

Recently, I was issued a very expensive and cool gun light. It was a high tech marvel. Once we mounted them on our rifles and took them on operations we soon discovered that in spite of all of the space shuttle technology the light offered, it suffered from a fatal flaw that made it an operational No-Go. When we hit our push to talk on our tactical radios, the light would give an unexpected and indiscrete ND. This experience acted to further reinforce what I have discovered over the years; simple, high quality tools are best!

High Lumens, simple circuitry and simple controls are the trifecta to a good light choice. For around a decade manufacturers have been pushing the strobe option. Personally, I am not a fan of strobe settings. Often getting this function to work requires more dexterity and thinking than one would want to spend operating any flashlight, much less one I am using in a tactical situation. My preference is; push a button, bright light on, release the button, bright light off.

Another technical consideration is the kind of light beam it produces. Does it have a tight beam or does it have a wide halo type projection? Consider the pros and cons. A tight beam concentrates light but may require the operator to move the light around a target area to see everything in a suspicious area. If speed is any kind of consideration this could result in some key visual information being missed, which could result in a bad shoot or possibly telegraph your location to an opponent that may be in a part of the room your light has not illuminated yet.

Think of it this way, you and your partner enter to clear a room and move to your point of domination; now there are two narrow light beams crossing back in fourth in the room and the only things being seen are what is directly in the light beam. The flip side to this coin is a wide halo light projection.

In the same scenario, you would get a lot of light in the room but quite possibly not as much ability to discriminate the details to determine whether a threat is actually a threat. There are lights that have a happy balance of a tight light cone with a good halo to facilitate seeing a broad area with enough horsepower to effectively discriminate and stun a potential threat as well as give enough peripheral light to the operator to use his sights effectively. It is within the previously described technical and performance parameters that drive the decision of what is a good combat light for me. If you combine the aforementioned requirements with a compact, streamlined and lightweight product, and you have good light to fight with.

(Editor's Note)

Many inexpensive, foreign made, LED lights offer a wide halo or field of view but are tremendously lacking in depth of penetration or distance. A reliable tactical light should allow you to clearly identify targets at distance; 25,

50, even 100 yard, not just five feet away. Buyer beware.

GUN LIGHTS vs. HANDHELD LIGHTS

I have given you my thoughts on what is required in a gun light and handheld tactical flashlight, now I want to stress the importance of having both of these items as well as a working proficiency with each. Having a light on your gun is very useful to say the least. But that is only one part of the solution in a low light environment.

One key concept you need to remember is that once you put a light on the gun it becomes part of that weapon, and we automatically limit the utility of that light. By this I mean you would not, and should not, use the light on your pistol to casually light up an alley or hall way without there being some sort of probable cause or defined threat.

To cover this situation or operational gap we need a light that doesn't have a deadly force element attached to it. As any police officer knows, you use a flashlight more than just about any tool you have. You are going to look at far more things than you are going to shoot. As such, it is critical that we augment our gun light with a safe alternative which is a hand held light. With that, let me give you some thoughts how we incorporate hand held lights into our combat system.

There are all kinds of hand held light techniques out there from which to choose to pair your pistol and light should the need arise. There is the Harries, Chapman, Ayoob, Rogers, FBI, Neck Index and I am sure several more. You can spend a huge amount of time training learning to use all these techniques and never get good at them all.

It is more practical to try out many and then choose a couple techniques to train with, and then practice. Remember to keep it simple. At Combat Shooting and Tactics (CSAT) we focus on two basic techniques that we have modified to work within our system and we end up playing the whole course with them. The key point is to choose techniques that can cover all the contingencies, keep them simple and train with them to a high degree of proficiency.

Training and practicing these skills should be methodical, start on the flat range getting used to simply turning the light on and off. Then work on using the light in a momentary mode while identifying a target. When you are comfortable with that particular point of performance, add in your live fire and work your marksmanship skills. Once you have established solid skills with each performance point, tie it all together: sparkle your target, discriminate, engage, turn off the light and move positions. After you have become proficient running through this engagement process, really start to push your discrimination skills.

CONCLUSION

As you start training for low light operations there are some simple but important things to remember. Using a light in a low light situation is a double edged sword. Not only are you illuminating your threat, but you are also identifying yourself to that threat. So, moving or establishing a covered position after you tip your hand by illuminating someone is an imperative point of performance in a gunfight.

For those of you who have trained with me before, you can see how basic shooting can easily become a complex mental process, especially if you are under stress. Once again, you will see that thinking through your situation and solving one problem at a time is just as important as good marksmanship. Your primary weapons system is your mind and your mindset.

In closing, these are the broad strokes of low light shooting and the points discussed should serve to give you a solid base to understanding the basics of the subject. We have talked about choosing our equipment and what to look for in a good combat light along with some historical anecdotes. We explored the effects low light has on our ability to discriminate threats and how to expand our reaction time while reducing the bad guys.

Finally, we spoke about the need for augmenting our gun lights with hand held lights as well as training with the tools we have chosen. My goal was to provide you a solid foundation that will solidly support the multitude of other low light topics and tactics should you decide to expand. Simple, reliable equipment chosen to maximize tactical advantage combined with good working knowledge of how and when to apply basic tactics will increase your chances of physical and professional survival exponentially.

*OODA LOOP- Developed Colonel John Boyd USAF during the Korean War as a way to regain the edge in the aerial war raging in the skies over that theater. Boyd decided that it was better to attack the enemy pilots thought process, rather than the enemy aircraft which at the time had better performance than the US F-86. His methodical approach of OBSERVE, ORIENT, DECIDE and ACT, got American fighter pilots inside the enemy's reaction loop and was instrumental in regaining control of the air space over Korea. By the end of the war US pilots enjoyed a 10-1 kill ratio over the Mig-15s.

-Shane Iversen is a retired US Army Master Sergeant with decades of real world experience. He is currently the Senior Instructor for CSAT Mobile Training Team. Contact them directly at www.CSATMTT.com

Smoke and Pryo

In the military, pyrotechnic signaling is commonplace. Generally, colored smoke is used in daylight and colored aerial flares or "star clusters" at night. When I was in the Marine Corps infantry, during peacetime training we reserved red smoke and red flares for emergency ceasefires and to indicate a medical emergency. Yellow, green, violet, and white smoke were used to mark an LZ, commence fire, shift fire, etc. The white smoke grenades we were issued produced the heaviest volume of smoke and were used for screening purposes to shield movement from the eyes of the enemy.

Colored flares or star clusters were used for signaling but produced little useful illumination for the people on the ground. For temporary illumination, a device called parachute flare could be launched from a handheld tube, we also had "illum" rounds for the M203 grenade launcher, mortars, and artillery. The "arty illum" was the largest and brightest.

Keeping with our discussion of the Patriot Fire Team, colored smoke or aerial flares could be used to signal other team members, particularly for medical emergencies or to call for help or draw attention to a problem.

I will give you a simple example. In the aftermath of a natural disaster, you name it, with the power out and law enforcement spread thin, community members will be responsible for the safety of their neighborhoods. You may have a large area to cover. Armed PFT members may be called upon to stand guard or to patrol in order to keep out looters and other vermin who would take advantage of the situation.

An easy way to call attention to a security problem at night, let other team mates and good guys know, would be to launch an aerial flare. Standard Operating Procedure (SOP) could be established that if a team member encountered looters or other vermin after dark they are to alert others by launching a flare. During hours of daylight colored smoke could be used to mark a trouble spot that requires team attention.

Naturally, smoke and flares could be used by PFT members to signal the need for assistance for security threats or medical emergencies. In the gravest extreme where PFT personnel needed to rescue and/or evacuate others in the midst of a hostile situation (urban riot) smoke could be used as a screen. No, smoke does not provide cover, but it does provide temporary concealment.

By this time many of you might be saying, "Smoke and flare advice is all well and good, but only the police and military have them." Not so says I. While the products might not be MilSpec, maritime rescue tools are readily available at most any store that sells boats or boating accessories.

Orion Signal is one of the biggest manufacturers of maritime rescue gear to include 12 gauge flares and launchers as well as 25mm signal flares and launchers. Orion produces colored rescue smoke as well. Most all products offered by Orion do indeed meet US Coast Guard standards. That fact is a positive as they are made to be water-resistant, meaning they will not get ruined by the rain.

During the last few years, many companies imported 26.5mm smoke and flare launchers and ammunition made in the former Soviet Republics. Our experience is that these work relatively well. We have had a couple of shells not ignite, but they are more readily available and less expensive than 37mm smoke and pyro.

Spikes Tactical makes a 37mm smoke/flare launcher called the "Havoc". The launcher can be mounted to a Picatinny rail or a specially designed stock. These are 'non-gun' devices so no ATF forms need to be filled out. In order to make the device more versatile, Spikes Tactical offers adapters to allow both 12-gauge signal flares and 26.5mm smoke and flares to be launched from the Havoc device.

We have used handheld white smoke grenades from a company called "Sport Smoke". Their "tactical smoke" grenades have a pull ring ignition and the ones we used produced an impressive amount of smoke and burned for at least a full minute. The only downside I can see is that they might be susceptible to moisture damage if not stored in a water-resistant container.

Chinese fireworks might seem like a cheap alternative, but they are just that "cheap". They are also susceptible to damage from moisture and are often hit and miss. Trying to light the fuse during a high stress emergency can be a recipe for failure.

Don't forget about Chemlights for marking positions or signaling. For the two people in the world who do not know what a "Chemlight" is, allow me a moment. A Chemlight is a sealed plastic tube that contains compounds that, when separated, are inert. To make light, you bend the plastic tube until the container inside cracks open. Shake the unit and the components mix and give off light for a certain amount of time.

MilSpec chemlights are the most expensive because they have a long shelf life and glow for up to 24 hours. Chinese Halloween toy chemlights are inexpensive but have a shorter shelf life and do not glow as bright or as long. Orion Signal makes "light sticks" that should prove more reliable than the holiday toy chemlights you find at Wal-Mart. Ameriglo chemlights are bit more expensive but the highest quality products you are likely to find.

Whichever products you end up with, it is important to have predetermined plans of action for smoke and flare signaling. Also, be sure that the pyro is spread out among team members and that everyone on the team understands how to use/activate the devices. You should not be trying to read directions during the adrenaline dump of an emergency.

Manual Signaling

One of the simplest and yet overlooked signal tools is the whistle. Yes, a whistle. That little device that you blow air into from which a loud, distinctive noise emanates. Whistles are invaluable for search and rescue. Yelling for help at the top of your lungs will quickly become exhausting. Blowing into a whistle requires little energy but the sound will travel for great distances.

Regarding team tactics, a whistle blast can be used to signal many things; commence movement or cease movement. It can indicate to others that there is a security threat or call their attention to a problem.

Next up on the simplicity scale is the signal mirror. A signal mirror is primarily considered a search and rescue tool, but it can be used to gain the attention of people at a distance. Naturally this is not as immediate as a radio call, but the signal mirror is not affected by wind or run by batteries.

If an immediate audible signal is necessary to warn or alert team members, discharging a firearm in rapid succession should gain their attention and indicate direction. Remember, one gunshot will alert the listener, a second and third will allow them to triangulate the direction from which the gunshots originated.

*Gunfire used as a signaling tool is naturally reserved for a crisis or emergency situation. Please do not confuse an audible signal for a "warning shot". We do NOT fire weapons at people as a warning. Deadly force rules apply.

⁇

Chapter 6: Leadership

Go to your emergency cupboard and take a look inside. If you are a prepared individual, you will see long term storage food, fresh water, medical supplies, and various comfort items.

Now walk over to your gun safe and open it. Again, I am guessing you will find defensive tools; guns, ammunition, and various tactical accessories.

Of all the emergency and tactical response items you have stocked up "just in case", there is one critical item that cannot be purchased and stored in a cabinet; leadership. Leadership in the United States of America is in desperately short supply and it is a trait that is essential in the aftermath of any disaster or crisis.

As you have this book in yours hands and have consumed the words to this point, I feel it is a safe bet that you have some aspirations to be a leader. Perhaps you do not consider yourself to be a leader of anyone or you could already be a boss with several employees. Maybe you are a husband or father and are the leader of your family. The great thing about leadership is that you do not have to wait for someone's permission to start exercising it. You can adopt and employ proven leadership traits on your own, no special title is required.

During this chapter I am going to dip back into the well of knowledge and information from which I learned to drink nearly thirty years ago; United States Marine Corps Leadership training. When I was in the Corps, shortly after a Marine became a Lance Corporal they were groomed to become a Non-Commissioned Officer (NCO). In addition to being mentored by experienced NCO's, young Marines were strongly encouraged to complete Marine Corps Institute courses for advancement. One MCI course required to achieve the rank of Corporal was "Leadership."

Marine Corps Leadership Traits

I once had the honor of serving as a member of the Marine Detachment stationed aboard the aircraft carrier USS Forrestal. The ladder (stairs for civilians) that lead out of our berthing area was painted Marine Corps red and on each rung a single word was painted in yellow (we didn't have scarlet and gold paint). Fourteen words were visible every time we ascended the ladder, they were the 14 USMC leadership traits.

Rather than paraphrase the leadership traits or attempt to restate them, I will instead offer them to you verbatim. Take a moment to digest each and every trait and consider where you are on your journey.

The 14 leadership traits are qualities of thought and action which, if demonstrated in daily activities, help Marines earn the respect, confidence, and loyal cooperation of other Marines. It is extremely important that you understand the meaning of each leadership trait and how to develop it, so as to know what goals to set as you work to become a good leader and a good follower.

JUSTICE

Definition: Justice is defined as the practice of being fair and consistent. A just person gives consideration to each side of a situation and bases rewards or punishments on merit.

Suggestions for Improvement: Be honest with yourself about why you make a particular decision. Avoid favoritism. Try to be fair at all times and treat all things and people in an equal manner.

JUDGMENT

Definition: Judgment is your ability to think about things clearly, calmly, and in an orderly fashion so that you can make good decisions.

Suggestions for Improvement: You can improve your judgment if you avoid making rash decisions. Approach problems with a common sense attitude.

DEPENDABILITY

Definition: Dependability means that you can be relied upon to perform your duties properly. It means that you can be trusted to complete a job. It is the willing and voluntary support of the policies and orders of the chain of command. Dependability also means consistently putting forth your best effort in an attempt to achieve the highest standards of performance.

Suggestions for Improvement: You can increase your dependability by forming the habit of being where you're supposed to be on time, by not making excuses and by carrying out every task to the best of your ability regardless of whether you like it or agree with it.

INITIATIVE

Definition: Initiative is taking action even though you haven't been given orders. It means meeting new and unexpected situations with prompt action. It includes using resourcefulness to get something done without the normal material or methods being available to you.

Suggestions for Improvement: To improve your initiative, work on staying mentally and physically alert. Be aware of things that need to be done and then to do them without having to be told.

DECISIVENESS

Definition: Decisiveness means that you are able to make good decisions without delay. Get all the facts and weigh them against each other. By acting calmly and quickly, you should arrive at a sound decision. You announce your decisions in a clear, firm, professional manner.

Suggestions for Improvement: Practice being positive in your actions instead of acting half-heartedly or changing your mind on an issue.

TACT

Definition: Tact means that you can deal with people in a manner that will maintain good relations and avoid problems. It means that you are polite, calm, and firm.

Suggestions for Improvement: Begin to develop your tact by trying to be courteous and cheerful at all times. Treat others as you would like to be treated.

INTEGRITY

Definition: Integrity means that you are honest and truthful in what you say or do. You put honesty, sense of duty, and sound moral principles above all else.

Suggestions for Improvement: Be absolutely honest and truthful at all times. Stand up for what you believe to be right.

ENTHUSIASM

Definition: Enthusiasm is defined as a sincere interest and exuberance in the performance of your duties. If you are enthusiastic, you are optimistic, cheerful, and willing to accept the challenges.

Suggestions for Improvement: Understanding and belief in your mission will add to your enthusiasm for your job. Try to understand why even uninteresting jobs must be done.

BEARING

Definition: Bearing is the way you conduct and carry yourself. Your manner should reflect alertness, competence, confidence, and control.

Suggestions for Improvement: To develop bearing, you should hold yourself to the highest standards of personal conduct. Never be content with meeting only the minimum requirements.

UNSELFISHNESS

Definition: Unselfishness means that you avoid making yourself comfortable at the expense of others. Be considerate of others. Give credit to those who deserve it.

Suggestions for Improvement: Avoid using your position or rank for personal gain, safety, or pleasure at the expense of others. Be considerate of others.

COURAGE

Definition: Courage is what allows you to remain calm while recognizing fear. Moral courage means having the inner strength to stand up for what is right and to accept blame when something is your fault. Physical courage means that you can continue to function effectively when there is physical danger present.

Suggestions for Improvement: You can begin to control fear by practicing self-discipline and calmness. If you fear doing certain things required in your daily life, force yourself to do them until you can control your reaction.

KNOWLEDGE

Definition: Knowledge is the understanding of a science or art. Knowledge means that you have acquired information and that you understand people. Your knowledge should be broad, and in addition to knowing your job, you should know your unit's policies and keep up with current events.

Suggestions for Improvement: Increase your knowledge by remaining alert. Listen, observe, and find out about things you don't understand. Study field manuals and other military literature.

LOYALTY

Definition: Loyalty means that you are devoted to your country, the Corps, and to your seniors, peers, and subordinates. The motto of our Corps is Semper Fidelis! (Always Faithful). You owe unwavering loyalty up and down the chain of command, to seniors, subordinates, and peers.

Suggestions for Improvement: To improve your loyalty you should show your loyalty by never discussing the problems of the Marine Corps or your unit with outsiders. Never talk about seniors unfavorably in front of your subordinates. Once a decision is made and the order is given to execute it, carry out that order willingly as if it were your own.

ENDURANCE

Definition: Endurance is the mental and physical stamina that is measured by your ability to withstand pain, fatigue, stress, and hardship. For example, enduring pain during a conditioning march in order to improve stamina is crucial in the development of leadership.

Suggestions for Improvement: Develop your endurance by engaging in physical training that will strengthen your body. Finish every task to the best of your ability by forcing yourself to continue when you are physically tired and your mind is sluggish.

(Suggestion Source: Strategic Leadership Studies website)

Because it was important to always be able to remember the basic leadership traits, the

acronym "J.J. DID TIE BUCKLE" was used to aid young Marines. Each letter in the acronym corresponds to the first letter of one of the traits. By remembering the acronym, you will be better able to recall the traits.

Parting Thoughts for Leadership Traits

Naturally, I would not expect you to master each and every leadership trait in one session. Instead, what I would challenge you to do is to take a two week, or 14-day, challenge. Each morning before you begin your day read one Marine Corps leadership trait, write it down or type it into your phone.

If you are genuinely serious about self-improvement, take 14 note cards and put one leadership trait with explanation on each. Place the stack where you will see it each morning. Read the top card aloud and then move it to the back of the stack. You can repeat the 14-day cycle until you have achieved the results you desire.

As you progress through each day look for ways or areas where you might be able to apply the trait of the day. Look for opportunities to apply your daily leadership trait. By the end of two weeks you should be on your way toward self-improvement and understanding the path to leadership.

This nation, and the world for that matter, is starving for leaders. You do not need to be a President or politician to be a leader. Hell, most of them are not leaders at all but popularity contest winners. Imagine how much better the United States of America would be if our elected employees had to first pass the Marine Corps Leadership training course.

Assignments and Tasking

Everyone has a role to play and the reason we work as teams is so that no person has to do it all themselves. When it comes to leadership, even the best officer in the world needs to divide up the work load. Generals Washington and Patton had deputies and assistants, and I don't mean aids to bring them coffee.

In the United States Army and Marine Corps, staff leadership tasks are assigned to numerous people who take instructions from, and report back to, the Commanding Officer. These designators are either (G) for general or (S) for staff. Sometimes these slots are a (J) rate for "joint" missions. Regardless of the letter at the beginning, the number designator indicates their duties. For simplicity sake, we will use the G series.

G1   Personnel

G2   Intelligence and Security

G3   Operations

G4   Logistics

G5   Plans

G6   Communications and Signals

G7   Training

G8   Finance/Resource Management

G9   Civil Affairs

It should be obvious that, depending on the size of the unit, some people may wear more than one "hat". Also, the operation might be such that not every "G" staff position is even necessary or they are rolled into one. For example, G3 and G5 could become one or G4 and G8 could be combined.

The Patriot Fire Team is not a battalion or regiment, so you might at first glance dismiss these as superfluous. Before you dismiss them completely, consider that each fire team member might do well with some task assignments.

Training, for instance, is a good example. With regards to training, one team member can be given the G7 director hat. Rather than having four guys coming up with training ideas, have one person do the research, scheduling etc.

For logistics you might have one team member tasked with finding good deals on ammunition or long term storage food. This could be as simple as the G4 guy sending a text or email to all the team members alerting them that "x" ammo company is running a sale on 9mm ball ammo. In our current condition as a nation, ammo sales are often short-lived.

You should get the idea by now. Also, you might want to mix it up annually and have members switch positions. Give people a mission and let them work it out.

Team Manual

Chapter 7: Team Tactics

Anyone can go to shooting course and learn how to safely operate a firearm and hit a target most of the time. During the aftermath of a crisis or an emergency situation, discharging a firearm may be only one small part of the overall survival plan. Yes, being able to hit your target on demand is important, that is a given.

I remember coming home on leave while on active duty in the Marines Corps and talking to some misguided acquaintances. Occasionally I would encounter guys from my old high school. Upon discovering that I had become a Marine, and under the influence of malted hops, some would say things akin to "Man, I can shoot a gun, I could do that." or "I'm a great shot, I'd be an awesome Marine."

What these boisterous and often loud-mouthed individuals failed to realize was that there was far more to being a United States Marine, or soldier for that matter, than "shooting a gun". They could not understand the physical and mental discipline that went into earning the title. Infantry training is about much more than simply aiming a rifle and pressing a trigger. During all phases of Basic training, followed by

Infantry training, you are taught and practice working as a team.

Being a Patriot Fire Team involves far more than four individuals who happen to own a few guns and some emergency supplies. Four men working as a team can accomplish far more than four individuals working on four different plans.

Team Building

As mentioned in the original Patriot Fire Team book, it is important that all the members of the team have similar training, a basic foundation. If you cannot attend training at the same time, at least take the same courses. For example, there are the Fighting Pistol or Fighting Rifle classes from Tactical Response or SOTG University's Beyond the Band Aid course. Naturally there are others.

The next step is to attend training that is geared around team tactics. Partner tactics classes can be found if you look. Small unit, fire team, training is more difficult to find but not impossible. Non-tactical team building suggestions are offered in the first PFT book as well.

Think of commercial training courses like a type of Boot Camp. Those programs lay the foundation to build upon. Everyone on the team will, at very least, have fundamental training so they can be expected to handle firearms in a safe and effective manner around other humans.

*Word of Caution: Cold Range/Empty Gun courses DO NOT teach you how to carry a loaded firearm amongst other humans in day to day environments. Cold Range training is about marksmanship and mechanics. Cold Range/Empty Gun training courses are not based upon teaching you to actually "carry" a firearm around other people.

Patrolling

One of the most fundamental jobs for an infantry soldier is patrolling. In the military you have three types of patrols; Combat, Recon, and Security. The Combat patrol is conducted with the purpose of seeking out and engaging the enemy. Basically you are looking for a fight and prepared to win it.

A Reconnaissance (recon) patrol is designed to stealthily discover and assess the enemy's location, numbers, assets, and possible intentions. Recon patrols attempt to avoid contact with the enemy. Information gathering is the key.

The Security patrol is designed to keep the enemy honest and to make it difficult for them to access or infiltrate our area of operation (AO). The Security patrol is conducted using varied routes and random times. It does little good to establish a set course and set time frame for a Security patrol. All the enemy would have to do is observe you twice and they could avoid your patrol.

A Security patrol is used to ensure the overall security of the perimeter surrounding your AO. For the Patriot Fire Team, your first concern will be the aftermath of a natural or manmade crisis. Standard law enforcement assets will be spread thin, communication with government emergency services difficult or non-existent, you are on your own.

Consider this scenario; in the aftermath of a disaster you have gathered your team and team families into a neighborhood area with a dozen or so houses. You know all the residents and they are on board with the survival and security plan. Unfortunately, the local thug element is using the advent of the crisis to rob, rape, and steal anything of value. How do you keep them out of your AO?

One tool in your toolbox is to conduct random Security patrols. Vehicle patrols (trucks, ATV's, snowmobiles, etc.) allow you to cover more ground but they eat precious fuel resources and vehicles can be seen and heard from a distance. Horseback patrols are valuable as they, again, allow you to cover more ground and they offer a raised field of view. However, in an urban area horses and tack are going to be difficult to come by.

More often than not, you will be on foot for your Security patrols. While foot patrols limit the distance you can cover in an allotted time, they do offer the benefit of being the stealthiest. A disciplined and trained team can move very quietly on patrol.

Security patrols can quickly become mundane and it is easy for team members to be lulled into a false sense of comfort. Perhaps you have conducted five, ten, maybe twenty patrols, all without incident. Now you become lax, start talking or making more noise during patrols. You get bored and your mind wanders.

Security is indeed boring, right up to the moment it becomes unexpectedly exciting. It takes personal discipline and quality leadership to ensure that a Security patrol is an effective use of time and resources, not just checking the blocks and going through the motions.

Your patrol might take ten minutes or an hour or more depending on the size of your AO. Before you take one step on the patrol, every member of the team needs to understand their role and responsibilities. Med gear, communication gear, passwords (if any), the location of other good guys in the area, weapons and personal equipment all must be addressed if the patrol is going to be effective.

A patrol is truly a very basic task, but it is also critical to the overall success of the mission. In the Marine Corps Infantry there are certain troop leading steps that should be considered. Referring back to my Rifle Squad Manual, allow me to highlight some of the steps.

The Five Paragraph Order is fundamental and for easy reference we use the acronym: SMEAC

Situation: Enemy activity (hostile forces), Friendly forces and activity

Mission: What is our clear and concise plan, what do we hope to accomplish?

Execution: How do we intend to accomplish our mission? What are the concept tasks, instructions, etc.

Administration: Rations, Water, Ammo, Medical gear

Commands and Signals: Challenge and Passwords, Communications gear to be used, predetermined signals, etc.

You might think this a bit overblown for a four-man Patriot Fire Team so let me give you an example of SMEAC from a practical standpoint.

Situation: Post-natural disaster, electrical power disabled for most all of the city/county, limited road access due to debris and flooding. Looting, theft, rape, and assault are ongoing in dense metropolitan areas. State, County and Local law enforcement are hampered and overwhelmed by number of calls for aid. State Guard Units are activating but not currently available. Community members must protect and care for each other.

Mission: Patrol residential neighborhood to discourage looting and criminal activity or detect and interrupt said activity.

Execution: Determine method of patrol (foot, ATV, Car/Truck, horseback), map out patrol route(s), determine patrol routine and times, members of patrol and their individual tasks.

What is the plan of action if hostile looters are encountered? Do you simply point guns at them and tell them to go away? What if the looters attack the patrol? What do you do if looters are caught in the act of rape, assault, theft, etc. Do you have plan for securing prisoners? Can you legally detain another citizen?

Administration: Does everyone have food and water? Do you need to take food or just water? Does everyone have basic gear: firearm, ammunition, load-bearing vest or pack, flashlight, foul-weather gear?

Commands and Signals: What time will you leave and expect to return and which friendly personnel are aware of your plans? What are your challenge and passwords for friendly personnel? You don't want a nervous armed sentry to shoot you thinking you are looter.

If you are using a vehicle and it breaks down how do you get another one? Who do you call? If your team runs into a large group of looters and are attacked, how do you call for relief or rescue? Do not dismiss that idea as paranoid. At this very moment drug cartels are running their product across the southern border using heavily armed squad-sized groups (10-12 men).

You can see how something as simple as driving around the neighborhood to discourage looting can become a serious undertaking if everything does not go as planned. What if someone on the team is injured? Who takes care of them and how do you get them back to the safe area?

Prior planning will eliminate panic and the need to make it up as you go along. Remember, if you have armed citizens operating in a crisis situation with the threat of looters/thugs, mistakes can be deadly. It is not unheard of for armed good guys to fire on each other in cases of mistaken identity.

Everyone on the team needs to understand the situation, mission, execution, administration, and commands and signals of the operation, even for something as simple as a security patrol.

Also every plan should have four (4) contingencies: Primary, Secondary, Tertiary, and Emergency.

Consider the patrol. Before you step off, everyone gathers around a map, overhead photographs (thanks Google Earth), a drawing, or sand table model. You must determine the Primary route of travel, a Secondary route if you run into obstacles, a Tertiary route if the secondary route is blocked, and an Emergency route to get back to safety.

Use your knowledge of the area and terrain to your advantage. You should know the areas that always flood after a storm, the marshes and swamps that do not seem like much for a glance at a map but are nearly impossible to navigate. If you live near the coast, the tide tables may be helpful.

If you live in the suburbs or out in the county, what are the most likely routes that car loads of assholes will take when they decide to come and steal from you? Are there intersections, bridges or other areas you can block to keep the urban vermin from getting to your family and neighbors?

*Special Note: Find and secure maps and overhead photos BEFORE the crisis happens. Good luck doing so when the power is out and the looting has begun. This is where good leadership will shine.

Also, your mobile phone and GPS are all well and good when things are working well. Every team member should possess and understand how to use a lensatic compass. Think of a compass as your analog GPS; it does not need a WiFi signal or batteries.

Getting back to the Four (4) contingencies, from a fighting stand point, your Primary weapon might be your rifle, Secondary your handgun, Tertiary is a gun you pick up off the ground from a friendly or hostile, Emergency could be your fixed blade knife.

By running through options and plans in your mind BEFORE you need to employ them, you eliminate the mental hesitation, confusion or vapor lock that comes when people encounter the unexpected. When everyone is on the same sheet of music you are far more likely to achieve success, despite the unforeseen. ▯

Chapter 8: Get Your Affairs in Order

Prior to an overseas deployment, Marine Corps Infantry Battalions go through a series of workups and checklists. Not only are the men expected to possess the appropriate gear for the mission and be well-trained, there are other less tactical areas that need attention.

Every man has their dental records updated and any required procedures taken care of. For instance, I had my two remaining Wisdom teeth removed prior to my deployment with the 6th Marines (the first two were removed during basic training). The middle of the jungle or desert is not the place to have tooth problems.

It was not that the Corps could not get dental attention for their men. Removing a man from his unit to travel to a rear area for medical or dental care leaves a gap in the team. We do everything humanly possible to minimize the need for such gaps.

I can recall briefings with our Platoon Leader and the admin pogues to ensure that our Serviceman's Group Life Insurance information was up to date and current. For single Marines that was pretty easy as they normally had only one benefactor; their parents.

The process for married men was a bit more complex. Wives needed to have access to bank accounts and contact information with unit's ombudsman. The wives of the Regimental, Battalion, and Company Commanders normally formed a support network for the enlisted men's wives.

Every man needed to feel assured that his family would be taken care of and secure while he was away. This would allow them to focus their full attention on the mission at hand. Naturally, unexpected issues would come up. Kids or spouses would get sick or end up in the hospital, parents and grandparents would pass. However, every effort was made to ensure that all domestic affairs were in order.

I had a conversation with my friend Tommy when we were deployed to the front lines during Desert Shield/Storm. Tommy remarked that he did not worry about his wife and newborn son because she was strong and could take care of herself. Sadly, Tommy was killed in Kuwait a couple of months after that conversation.

After we returned to the states I wrote Tommy's wife a long letter and told her of the pride he had when speaking of her and the strength he was sure that she possessed. He was the only man in Charlie Company, 1/6 to die during Operation Desert Storm.

My experience is not necessarily unique. Military units throughout history have had ways to prepare their men for war and extended absence from home. It is no mystery that men who are constantly fretting about domestic affairs cannot focus their energy on the mission at hand. It is one thing to dream of going home, it is quite another to constantly worry that your family is experiencing hardship and hunger while you are away.

As a member of a Patriot Fire Team, you must ask yourself whether or not your absence will put your family in jeopardy or undue hardship. Does your wife have access to the money she needs to pay the mortgage or rent? Is there ample food in the house?

You might be saying "I'm not a soldier, I don't go away on deployments." If your team, community, or state needed your assistance during a crisis, would all be well at home for a few days? What if a few days turned into a week or more? Can you step out of your front door to face the ever present evil of our world feeling assured that your family will be taken care of if you should never be able to return?

When it comes to getting your affairs in order, my friend, James Yeager, addressed that issue thoroughly in his book; "High Risk Civilian Contracting: Working in a War Torn World." (Available on Amazon) While you might not be a contractor working overseas, much of what James has to say is the section entitled "Pre-Deployment Preparation" has bearing on the Patriot Fire Team member. Rather than paraphrase, I decided to include the entire section for your consideration. (Yes, naturally this was reprinted with the full permission from the publisher and author.)

Pre-Deployment Preparation

From "High Risk Civilian Contracting" by James Yeager

"I fear not the man who has practiced 10,000 kicks once, but I fear the man who has practiced one kick 10,000 times." - Bruce Lee

Preparation for this journey begins long before the opportunity ever presents itself. In the days, weeks, months, and years preceding this adventure, you will need to be gathering both knowledge and skill. You should be conditioning your mind and your body. It is a long journey. It's time to get started.

Financial Preparation

Now that you're certain that you've got the job, you want to prepare to depart. There are a few things that you need to take care of before you leave. In most cases, your pay will come monthly, and as a subcontractor, you might be asked to submit an invoice for your services each month. Your company will typically have a form for you to fill out but you should be careful to keep track of the time you spend working.

What you should be prepared for, however, is not being paid for at least two or maybe three months. Why so long? Here's the reason: you must first work a full month before you submit your first invoice. Then, it could take a couple of weeks or even a month before your company processes your invoice and you get paid. I would strongly suggest that before you leave, you have enough money in the bank to cover your bills for at least three months. This will ensure that while you are away, you can still cover all your financial responsibilities without going into arrears and possibly affecting your credit and even your continued employment. Bad credit scores strongly affect your ability to get and maintain a security clearance.

I also suggest consulting with a financial professional prior to deploying. You need to sit down with a competent accountant (be sure to vet them) and get some sound financial advice. This next point I cannot stress enough: do not try to deceive the Internal Revenue Service (IRS). If you get a good accountant, they will give you many ways to legally reduce your tax burden. They may tell you to incorporate or give you other investment or retirement plans to help shield you from excessive taxation. In general, you will be extremely well-paid for your work as a security contractor, and the temptation to try to hide or conceal your income might be strong, but do not try to do this. You want to survive the combat zone so you can go home, not to a federal prison cell.

Some people might say, "I thought if I worked out of the country, then my pay is tax free?" Under certain circumstances, and depending on the amount of money that you earn, that statement may well be true. Your accountant will be able to tell you what part of your pay is tax-free, or whether all of it is, or whether none of it is. Either way, the money you pay an accountant should have two rewards: one, that you keep as much of your money as is legally possible and two, that you do not have to worry about the Internal Revenue Service coming for their share long after you have spent it. You will also want to talk to him about the Self

Employment Tax to make sure he is well-read on the subject.

If you do need to incorporate, you are going to need an attorney (be sure to vet him too!). This is a good thing because an attorney is on the list of people you should visit before you leave anyway. While you are there, take care of a few things; if you don't have a Will, you need to get one before you leave. Be sure to get advice on a Living Will, so your family knows what you want done if you become dependent on life support. You may also want to give a spouse or a family member a Power of Attorney or a Limited Power of Attorney.

A qualified attorney can tell you the difference and can give you the advice you will need. You want a good lawyer to ensure that your powers of attorney, living will, will, and the contracts you sign are legal and bulletproof. Just like with a good accountant, a good attorney is almost worth his weight in gold (depending on how hefty your attorney might be!)

You'll want to have a lawyer who specializes in corporate law and contracts look over your employment contract when you get one and have him explain it to you. This will cost you money before you start working, but it can save you heartache and hassle further down the line.

You will also need to get current information on how civilian security contractors are affected by the Uniform Code of Military Justice (UCMJ) and how the laws of the United States of America and the country you are going to apply to while you are doing security work. Don't put this off— no one wants to end up in prison, much less a foreign prison.

So, how are you going to get all the cash you're going to make back home? Do you plan on carrying it home in large black duffle bags? While certainly dramatic, I feel that that's just a bit unsafe. I suggest being prepared to be paid by a direct deposit on a monthly basis. For this, you will need to know your bank's SWIFT code (essentially a zip code for banks). Knowing that information will help to get your money to your bank as fast as possible. You will also need to know your bank's routing number and your account number. You can call your bank or pay them a visit in order to get the SWIFT code, and you can get your routing and account numbers off the bottom of a check (be sure to know which is which). Those three numbers will insure that any money sent to you will be received as smoothly as possible.

My suggestion to anyone before they go over is to have three months of your current salary in your bank before you leave. The pay process typically begins and the end of each month. Let's say you arrive on the 4th. You work until the 30th and the pay sheets are submitted. It will be 7-15 days at LEAST before the money shows up in your account. It could be 30 days and in some cases longer. That's a minimum of 33 days, if you're lucky, and a maximum of 56 days, if you're not.

Having a 90-day supply of money in the bank for your family makes it easy for you to sleep at night. The last thing you need to be worrying about on a dangerous mission is the bills back at home.

Life insurance is another thing to consider. You should understand that in most cases, if you have a long-standing life insurance policy, it should cover you. Make sure. Generally speaking, though, any new life insurance policies that you might add to your coverage will not. As a matter of fact, you most likely will not be able to even get additional coverage if your insurance company knows what you are about to do and where you are going. The same rule applies to your health insurance.

Medical Preparation

While you are out making office visits, take a trip over to your doctor's office (be sure to call ahead for an appointment) and get a check-up; while you're there, be sure to get copies of all of your medical records. If you have access to a computer and scanner, scan them into the computer and save them in a digital format, like a .PDF or .JPG. You might have to go to your local Health Department to get a copy of your immunization record. Do this, and scan that record into the computer as well. Don't forget to check the Center for Disease Control (CDC) website for information about what vaccines are recommended for travelers headed to the part of the world where you'll be working.

If you are on prescription medications, explain to your doctor where you are going and what you will be doing there. If you are on a specific work/leave rotation (90 days on/30 days off), he will need to know so that he can write you a prescription to cover the amount of medication you will need. You will want to get a prescription to cover your entire trip, and a little extra as well. Depending on where you are going in the world, it may be very difficult to get your prescription refilled and if it is possible to get a prescription filled, the quality of the drugs you receive could be suspect.

The last stop you should make is at the dentist's office. Drop in for a visit and stay for a thorough checkup and cleaning. The last place in the world you want to have a toothache is while you are working in a third-world country that has inadequate dental care. If you have filings, be sure to stop at your local pharmacy and get a small container of temporary tooth filling. It doesn't take up much room and it is great insurance against a toothache, which can make even the toughest security contractor completely mission-incapable.

Documents

You should buy a small flash-based memory stick (also called a flash drive, USB stick, etc.) Use the memory stick you've bought to store all your scanned medical records, immunization records, copies of your passport / driver's license / Will / Living Will, information about your life insurance policy, your personal address book, your bank account information, and any other important documents. Be sure to get a memory stick that is password-protected and guard it with your life. Do not let this memory stick out of your possession as the information it contains can easily be used by unscrupulous individuals to steal your identity. However, if you get into a situation where you are separated from your critical personal information, then this little bit of insurance will pay off in spades.

I suggest having color copies of the photo page of your passport made; be sure to carry these while traveling. If your passport is stolen, this will make it easier for you to replace it. No worries though; you did get the second passport like I told you to do, right? The color photocopy lets the US Embassy replace your passport with a minimum of hassle. A .JPG file of the same on the memory stick is good idea as well. Remember to protect it!

It is possible, if you are computer savvy, to have your critical files stored online in a secure manner. This can be a backup to your thumb drive. Don't rely solely on this method because you may be in an area that does not have reliable or secure access to the Internet. You need to ensure that you use a secure memory stick and always use a password of at least 12 characters, including numbers and symbols. Use a longer password if you can remember it. You don't want anyone to be able to randomly guess your password, so make it as complex as possible to prevent this.

Finally, you need to ensure that your critical documents are secure, yet available, stateside as well. If the only copy of your Will burns up with you, it is pretty useless now, isn't it? Get a safe deposit box at your local bank and leave the key with your lawyer or some other trustworthy person. Keep the original copies of your important documents in the safety deposit box and carry high-quality photocopies on your person. Just like with firearms, where two is one and one is none, be sure to have multiple copies of your important documents stored in several places so that you'll always be able to have access to them when you need them.

- James Yeager, HRCC

Patriot Fire Team

Preserving the Republic
Four Men at a Time

Paul G. Markel

Dedication

This book is dedicated to the memory of Cary McClelland, the grand patriarch of my mother's family. The McClelland family fled their native Scotland in the mid 1700's to Ireland in an attempt to escape British tyranny. In 1776 Cary again attempted to escape British tyranny by leaving Ireland and taking the long journey to the colonies in America.

Arriving in Philadelphia, Pennsylvania in April of 1776, Cary joined Geo. Washington's newly formed Continental Army as a Pennsylvania Rifleman of the Pennsylvania Line. He served and fought in the Battles of Long Island and White Plains. Cary's unit crossed the Delaware River Christmas night 1776 to take Trenton from the Hessian occupiers and then a week later they took the strategic town of Princeton from the British Army. The entire force then wintered at Valley Forge.

In 1777 Cary fought in the Battles of Brandywine and Germantown. After serving one year and nine months he received an honorable discharge. The McClellands settled in Greene County, PA after the war and many became rifle-makers. Upon his application for pension, Cary was granted a plot of land in the newly settled state of Ohio near Mt. Vernon. He and many others of my kin are laid to rest in the Bell Church Cemetery, Knox County, Ohio.

I would also like to honor Charles McClelland, my maternal grandfather and Patriot in his own right. In 1941 at the tender age of 17, Charles joined the United States Navy. After graduating from boot camp and "A" School, he was stationed aboard the USS Helena, a cruiser, homeported at Pearl Harbor, territory of Hawaii.

On the morning of December 7, 1941 Charles was at the front of the ship raising the Union Jack when his ship was hit by a bomb from an attacking Japanese aircraft. The explosion threw him into the air and when he landed on the steel deck his leg was broken.

By the time he had recuperated and returned to active service, the Helena had been repaired. My grandfather went to sea again and his battle group took part in the campaigns and naval battles to take Guadalcanal. The ship fought in the Battle of Kula Gulf and after an engagement with Japanese destroyers was sunk by enemy torpedoes.

Charles was one of a small number of survivors to be rescued from the Japanese held island of Vella Lavella. Returning to the United States to recover from malaria, he spent the remainder of his time assigned to the USS Missouri. He returned home with an honorable discharge in 1946 to his young wife, my beautiful grandmother, Betty.

I sat at my grandfather's feet from a young age as he told me tales of World War II and Navy life. He was the one who located a copy of Cary McClelland's original US Army pension application on file in the Knox County Courthouse in Mt. Vernon, Ohio and educated me to our family's history. It is my sincere hope to honor these men through the effort I put into this book.

Paul G. Markel July, 2014

"The name of American, which belongs to you in your national capacity, must always exalt the just pride of patriotism more than any appellation derived from local discriminations."

George Washington from his Farewell Address

Preface

First, I would like to express sincere appreciation to you for taking the time to begin digesting this work. Conventional publishing wisdom has offered that in order to be "popular" or a "best seller" the author should dumb down their work to a sixth grade reading level. I would offer that a sixth grade reading level today and a sixth grade reading level in 1780 are decidedly different with the education and comprehension nod going to the Eighteenth Century.

As a nation, the United States of America suffers multiple ailments, of which intellectual laziness is one. The deliberation of using 'small words' and short sentences does little but support, or at very least enable, that self-imposed mental handicap. I will have none of that silliness here. Words will be used when and where they are deemed appropriate, even if they have origins in Latin or are multisyllabic.

Your benevolent author is working on his fifth decade here on Earth and still considers himself, not only to be a student of the gun but, a student of the spoken and written word. If this old dog can park his ego and attempt to broaden his horizons, then certainly you can as well.

Facts will be checked and where warranted quotes offered and sourced. Nonetheless, this text has been compiled as an expression of the author's thoughts and opinions based upon his experience serving this nation as a United States Marine, a Law Enforcement Officer, an Executive Protection Agent, and professional Small Arms and Tactics Instructor during the last thirty years.

I often chuckle to myself when someone offers the advice to approach this topic or that without any preconceived notions. From a practical and realistic standpoint, few people, even Kindergarteners, can approach a subject with zero preconceived ideas or notions.

From the moment you are born you begin to learn and you are directly influenced by the world around you and the circumstance into which you were delivered. No one is a blank slate and you really would not want to be. I should not have to take the time to teach you that fire is hot, knives are sharp and you should not stick your fingers in the wall socket.

Instead of suggesting that you attempt to consume the material contained herein like a dry sponge or Bruce Lee's proverbial empty cup, I would ask that you be intellectually honest with yourself and consider that you are a student. As a willing pupil you will seek out various viewpoints, ideas and concepts that you may have never previously considered. As a point of fact, that aforementioned thought process is how you should approach every training course or formalized education exercise.

With all of that said, grab a pen or highlighter, you are going to want to take notes and underline certain quotes. Brew a pot of premium coffee (life is too short for cheap coffee) and, if you still live in Free America, light a quality hand-rolled cigar (ladies are invited as well) sit back and enjoy the ride.

PGM 2014

Introduction

In modern America, there are myriad men and women who inherently understand that the world is a dangerous and imperfect place. These folks realize that it is their responsibility to prepare for the safety and defense of their homes and families. Consequently, many of these people attempt to do it all on their own. While a noble pursuit, this situation often leads to frustration and occasionally a feeling of loneliness or hopelessness. "Am I the only one out there trying to do the right thing?" is a common thought.

Every man and woman needs occasional support and affirmation. Try as we might, we cannot do it all on our own and we should not have to.

The Patriot Fire Team is not some secret militia or fringe organization with tin-foil hats. The group is meant to consist of four individuals who have pledged to support and defend their families and communities. While doing so they will support the Constitution of the United States of America and its Bill of Rights. Each member has pledged to provide support and encouragement to the others whenever and wherever that support may be needed.

The more information we have access to and the larger the number of delivery systems for that so-called information, the greater the effect of state sponsored disinformation and media inspired think-speak. Consider the following.

The term "Militia" is laced throughout most every one of the founding documents. Read the Bill of Rights, for instance1. As recently as 1902 we see The Dick Act of 1902, sponsored by Ohio Representative Charles Dick, also referred to as the Efficiency of the Militia Act. In that bill three armed bodies were discussed for the protection and defense of the United States of America; the U.S. Army, the National Guard, and the Militia. The law went on to state that "every able-bodied male citizen of the respective States, resident therein, who is aged eighteen years and under the age of forty-five years, shall be enrolled in the militia."2

Militias were as much a part of the fabric of Colonial American society as fishing, farming, silver and blacksmithing. The leaders of local militia groups were not fringe kooks, but genuine civic leaders. In 1776, the leaders of local militias and "training bands" were prominent landowners, physicians, attorneys, and men of the church. It was quite common for your Church Deacon to also be a Captain in the local training band.3

Today, thanks to a decades old effort to besmirch and marginalize the term "militia" it has taken on a pejorative connotation. Even those schooled in the historical precedent of the use of the militia and training band fear to use the words for fear of being painted as "radical" or "fringe".

Citizen soldiers or armed citizens who were organized for the defense of their communities predate the American Revolution. In his book "Paul Revere's Ride" author David Hackett Fischer enumerates the history of the "training band". Hackett explains that the Massachusetts Training Bands comprised of citizen soldiers could be historically referenced as far back as 1645, more than one hundred years prior to the Declaration of Independence.

To put it quite simply, responsible citizens understood that it was indeed the duty of the able-bodied members of the community to be armed and prepared to defend themselves, their neighbors and their homes. This was not some insane anti-government movement, quite the contrary. In the British Colonies the organization of Training Bands often occurred as direct order of the King and Parliament, ergo the government. Imagine that, the sitting government instructing the citizens to be armed and trained for the defense of the nation?

As you sit and peruse this text in the 21st Century, the idea of the militia or training band may seem as foreign to you as shoeing a horse or digging a privy out behind your house. Certainly we, as a modern society, have long since surpassed the need to organize able-bodied men for the defense of the community. That is the responsibility of the government many would argue.

You might think that the previous assertions were fact if not for evidence to the contrary. The United States Supreme Court ruled that the police (the government) do NOT have the duty to protect citizens as individuals, only society in a general sense.4 This ruling has been reiterated by State Supreme Courts as recently as 2013 when the New York Supreme Court held the state harmless when police officers failed to stop a man from being brutally stabbed multiple times even though they saw the action taking place.

Although the legal concept has been cited numerous times, the Warren v. District of Columbia ruling is the case most often cited as precedent. Even if the Supreme Court did indeed hold that the state had a constitutional duty to protect all citizens as individuals, from a practical standpoint that task often proves impossible in the aftermath of natural and manmade disasters.

The Rodney King Verdict in 1992 sparked a manmade disaster in the greater Los Angeles, California area. Agents of the state battled with armed gang members while thousands upon thousands of residents were left to fend for themselves against roaming mobs of looters. Those looters engaged in theft, arson, robbery, rape, and even murder. The good intentions of the Los Angeles Police Department and LA County Sheriff could not protect everyone.

More recently, during the aftermath of Hurricane Katrina, residents of the greater New Orleans area witnessed a complete breakdown of society, as again, roving bands of criminals and drug gangs took control of the city for nearly a week's time. Thousands of businesses and homes were looted, ransacked and burned. The jury is still out on the total number of rapes and murders that took place in the Crescent City.

It was not until thousands of law enforcement officers armed with black rifles flooded into southern Louisiana from all points that order was restored and the rebuilding of New Orleans could begin. Yes, I know of this first hand as I arrived in New Orleans five days after the levees broke. I witnessed it all with my own eyes.

Sadly, but predictably, in the aftermath, post-Katrina crime numbers were deliberately downplayed to support the image of victimization for the entire area. Add the more recent events in Ferguson, Missouri and Baltimore, Maryland, to the list of lawlessness where citizens were left on their own.

With all of the above in mind, your humble author came up with the idea of the Patriot Fire Team. Allow a moment of elaboration.

The foundation unit of the United States Marine Corps Infantry, with whom I served, is not the Company, Battalion, or even the Squad. No, the base unit is the Fire Team. A Fire Team consists of four individuals; a Fire Team Leader, Automatic Rifleman, Assistant Automatic Rifleman, and Rifleman in order of rank from first to last. It is the responsibility of each man in the Fire Team to know the job of the man above him and to be able to assume that position at any point in time. Every member of the Fire Team is tasked with mutual support of the others. They share the load when it comes to both defensive and offensive operations. No man can cover all areas or do all the work themselves. Working as a unit, the four-man team is stronger and more effective than any four men acting as individuals could hope to be.

Introduction Footnotes

1   Bill of Rights, United States Constitution, 1791

2   "Efficiency of the Militia Act" H.R. 11645 U.S. Library of Congress, 1902

3   "Paul Revere's Ride" David Hackett Fischer, Oxford University Press, 1995

4   Warren v. District of Columbia, US Supreme Court No. 02-7120

Chapter One - Cover the Basics

Before you run out and purchase an AR-15 and a thousand rounds of ammunition, you should be sure all of the bases are covered. In the military we often refer to the basic necessities as "beans, bullets, and Band-Aids."

It does not matter how many guns or how much ammunition you own if you do not have a day's worth of clean drinking water or food. The greatest armies in the world have been defeated by bad weather or lack of food and water. Napoleon and Hitler had tons of bullets and powder but were ultimately defeated by foul weather. You cannot wrap yourself in your rifle to stave off the cold and you cannot eat your ammunition.

This book is not a primer for either guerrilla or conventional warfare; the purpose is to support a secure and fully functional community. Your community cannot survive if the people do not have their most basic needs met. In case you missed the point, relying on an external source, the state, for daily needs is not the aim of the Patriot Fire Team.

Let's start with the very basics, and I mean the foundation that each and every man and woman needs to have regardless of geographic location or ethnic origin. Abraham Maslow had it pretty well figured out and we will defer to his explanation during the next few pages.

In the modern world the word 'needs' is too often substituted for wants. You don't need a 42-inch flat screen TV, you want it. You want the latest iPhone; you don't need it. For those of you who never took Psyche 101 in college, or slept through the course, let me take a moment to introduce you to Abraham Maslow. A psychologist by trade, Maslow set out to understand what motivates humans to do what they do.

Maslow introduced his first "Hierarchy of Needs" in 19431. In this hierarchy he explained that, regardless of who they were or where they lived, all humans had certain physiological and psychological needs and that these needs built upon each other to allow the person to reach their ultimate potential. The Hierarchy of Needs is most often explained or displayed as a pyramid. The basic and most fundamental needs are at the base and more elusive psychological needs are at the top.

Understanding the Hierarchy of Needs

Starting at the base of the pyramid you have Biological/Physiological needs; air, water, food, warmth, sexual release and sleep. Next up is Safety; protection from the elements, security and /or freedom from fear, order, limits, and stability. Number three of the five levels are Social needs; belonging, affection and love; from family, friends and romantic relationships.

Second from the top of the needs pyramid is Esteem; achievement, mastery, independence, status, dominance, prestige, self-respect and respect from others. Lastly, at the top is Self-Actualization; realizing personal potential, self-fulfillment, seeking personal growth and peak experiences.

As would be expected, over the years, other psychologists and psychiatrists have debated the structure of the hierarchy of needs and its components. However, regardless of your opinion on the subject, it would seem obvious that a man cannot become a master architect or artist if he spends all of his time foraging for food and seeking shelter from the weather. Consider the average fifteen-year-old boy. It's difficult, if not impossible, for them to seek mastery and independence when their brains are consumed with thoughts of fifteen-year-old girls.

Can a man or woman focus on taking their business to the next level if there is domestic discord in their home? How many times have you heard the advice to "leave your home life at home"? Divorce, financial troubles, etc. all distract from the mission or career. Understanding this, those in the military or government will often lose their "Top Secret" security clearances based upon domestic troubles.

Needs in the Modern World

Sadly, few in today's society understand the Hierarchy of Needs or how each level supports the others. When people get the "prepping bug" they either don't know where to start or will stop at the base level.

Folks will go out and buy a six-month supply of freeze-dried food and call it good. Many will neglect the tools and skills needed to provide security for that aforementioned food. Others will go out and purchase a handgun and ammunition but they don't even have two days' worth of food in their cupboards at home.

An even more sinister and dangerous situation occurs when adults in society look to someone else for their fundamental Physiological and Safety needs. With food, water, and shelter provided by some faceless government bureaucracy, many people never learn to secure these things for themselves. What is worse, if there is ever an interruption in these social programs, the results are disastrous and the recipients, rather than step up and provide for themselves, devolve into a foraging animal state. I submit the Greater New Orleans area, post-Katrina, as Exhibit A.2

Examining the Hierarchy pyramid, we see that the higher needs are built upon the base needs. Some social engineers would offer that by having government social programs provide the foundational needs of the pyramid the recipient is free to focus on the upper levels of love and affection, achievement and mastery, independence and dominance in their career field or any field of endeavor.

What the aforementioned social architects ignore, whether by being naïve or through deliberation and design, is the fact that each individual must build their own pyramid. Self-respect, achievement and sense of belonging cannot be handed out in a food line. All of the aforementioned needs are products of individual struggle, effort and desire. Removing challenges and obstacles from an individual does not increase self-actualization and self-respect, it handicaps and stifles it. Never having learned to build the foundation of the pyramid, the individual flounders without order or structure, meaning or purpose.

21st Century Prepping

When the individual rediscovers Maslow or understands the hierarchy of needs for the first time, they realize what is required to build a "needs" pyramid with a solid foundation. You should understand that you cannot skip steps in the building process. Healthy family and romantic relationships are difficult to maintain if there is no stability in the food and shelter department. A person cannot reach self-fulfillment and seek personal growth and peak experiences if there is constant struggle at home.

Having taken the steps to store ample food and water, as well as safety and security tools, the individual can focus their attention on financial security and solvency. When they are financially secure people can focus on excelling in their career fields and achieving higher and loftier goals.

A person who has a mastery of their career field can advance to newer and more focused achievements. That person can mentor and provide opportunities to others. A person with a solid, well-built needs pyramid can focus on philanthropy and become a blessing to society, not a burden.

Parting Thoughts

Abraham Maslow's parents immigrated to the United States from Russia and he was the first of seven children. He lived through the Great Depression, arguably the most difficult financial time in U.S. history up until the modern era. The people who lived through, and survived, the Great Depression learned hard lessons about personal preparation and thrift; they learned the perils of indebtedness.

The great irony of our time is that our grandparents and great-grandparents survived hardship and went without only to raise a successive generation that has little understanding of genuine need or want. As we gaze out at the American landscape we see a society with seemingly no understanding of Maslow's Hierarchy of Needs or the importance of building that pyramid.

What you must ask yourself is this, how is your pyramid coming along? Is your foundation solid or built upon the fragile sand of some faceless social program? Is your pyramid built on endless credit card debt? To loosely quote Robert Plant,

...if the stores are all closed, with a word will you get what you came for?

With regards to the Patriot Fire Team, from the very beginning each member should inquire of others as to their state of readiness and supply of food and water. Remember, we support and encourage each other.

This is not some paranoid prepper conspiracy, it is life. Our parents and grandparents had homes with pantries and fruit cellars. They stocked them with food, not because they were paranoid whackos but because they knew that everyone in the house needed to eat each and every day.

In the case of most of our grandparents, at least mine, they always tried to make sure they had more than enough food so that they could feed visiting friends and family if the need arose. My grandmother is 89 years old, and today if you entered her home the first thing she would do is offer you something to drink and to eat. That is the way they were raised.

The primary question you must ask yourself is; are you and your family prepared to be a blessing or a burden? If you say you cannot afford "extra" food my first response would be that you cannot afford not to have ample food.

I would also suggest you look around your home and consider what is a want versus what is a need.

Chapter 1 Footnotes

1   "Motivation and Personality" Abraham Harold Maslow, Robert Freger, Harper and Rowe, 1987

2   "Relief Workers Confront 'Urban Warfare': Violence disrupts evacuation, relief efforts in New Orleans" CNN.com September 1, 2005Patriot Fire Team

Chapter Two - The Citizen is the Boss

"If ye love wealth better than liberty, the tranquility of servitude than the animated contest of freedom, go from us in peace. We ask not your counsels or arms. Crouch down and lick the hands which feed you. May your chains sit lightly upon you, and may posterity forget that you were our countrymen!" - Samuel Adams, founding member of the Sons of Liberty

There really is no point continuing with this text if we do not set some historical ground rules. Why fight if you do not know or understand that for which you are fighting? Yes, there are some who argue just for the sake of arguing, but that it not our intent. If you legitimately consider yourself an American Patriot, you must first have a solid understanding of what it is to be a United States Citizen.

Your place of birth may have been a happy accident or you may reside as a citizen of the United States of America by purpose and design. Regardless, if you hold true to the founding principles upon which this nation was built, you should understand that you have an opportunity not afforded to the vast majority of humans who have been born on this Earth since the dawn of time.

I have no intention of rehashing your Junior High American History class by discussing Pilgrims and the tale of Jamestown. Instead, we will consider and examine the political thought of the American Revolution and the history and precedent that the founders cited when creating the greatest experiment in self-governance that the world has ever known.

Declaration of Independence (presented to the people on July 4, 1776)

When in the Course of human events it becomes necessary for one people to dissolve the political bands which have connected them with another and to assume among the powers of the earth, the separate and equal station to which the Laws of Nature and of Nature's God entitle them, a decent respect to the opinions of mankind requires that they should declare the causes which impel them to the separation.

Note: the authority that the framers cited was Natural Law and the Laws of Nature's God (capitalized deliberately). The authority to break the political bands holding them to Great Britain came from the fact that they considered themselves to have "separate and equal

154

station". This is essential to understand. The framers declared that the citizens of the colonies had "equal station" to those in parliament and that they were not, therefore, a subservient or a peasant class.

When considering Natural Law and Rights, John Adams, who was an accomplished attorney and statesman before he became the President, once wrote of these Rights:

They are principles of Aristotle and Plato, of Livy and Cicero, and Sidney, Harrington, and Locke; the principles of nature and eternal reason; the principles on which the whole government over us now stands. It is therefore astonishing, if anything can be so, that writers who call themselves friends of government, should in this age and country be so inconsistent with themselves, so indiscreet, so immodest as to insinuate a doubt concerning them.[1]

You must remember that our founding fathers had a far greater attention span than we today and tended to use a copious amount of words to make the point. The point, nonetheless, that Adams was making was that for any man to argue against Natural Law and the Rights of Man was beyond imagination. So self-evident were man's rights as citizens that they dated back to the times of Plato and Aristotle.

Natural Law and the Natural Rights of Man were a common thread throughout speeches, sermons, pamphlets, newspaper articles, letters and orations delivered during the revolutionary period in the colonies from the 1760's right up to when the first shot was fired on Lexington green on April 19, 1775. Though many founders differed over the methods and machinations of separation from Mother England, few, if any, denied that all citizens of the British Colonies had the God-given right to pursue their own destiny as they saw fit.

We hold these truths to be self-evident, that all men are created equal, that they are endowed by their Creator with certain unalienable Rights, that among these are Life, Liberty and the pursuit of Happiness.

That verbiage borrowed from the Virginia Declaration of Rights by Thomas Jefferson;

Section 1. That all men are by nature equally free and independent and have certain inherent rights, of which, when they enter into a state of society, they cannot, by any compact, deprive or divest their posterity; namely, the enjoyment of life and liberty, with the means of acquiring and possessing property, and pursuing and obtaining happiness and safety.

Again, we note the reference to equal creation by their "Creator" (capitalized intentionally). "Unalienable Rights" are those which not only cannot be arbitrarily taken away, but cannot be surrendered. "Life, Liberty and the pursuit of Happiness", nowhere does it say a right to equality of outcome or the right to be free from discomfort, pain, suffering or poverty.

— That to secure these rights, Governments are instituted among Men, deriving their just powers from the consent of the governed,

Once more we see the affirmation and acknowledgement that Governments although instituted among Men, nonetheless derived their power from the direct consent of the people, the citizen. This once more denies the existence of a hereditary ruling class or oligarchy.

— That whenever any Form of Government becomes destructive of these ends, it is the Right of the People to alter or to abolish it, and to institute new Government, laying its foundation on such principles and organizing its powers in such form, as to them shall seem most likely to affect their Safety and Happiness. Prudence, indeed, will dictate that Governments long established should not be changed for light and transient causes; and accordingly all experience hath shewn that mankind are more disposed to suffer, while evils are sufferable than to right themselves by abolishing the forms to which they are accustomed. But when a long train of abuses and usurpations, pursuing invariably the same Object evinces a design to reduce them under absolute Despotism, it is their right, it is their duty, to throw off such Government, and to provide new Guards for their future security.

The above section states, for the public record, that when any Form of Government becomes destructive, the citizens do not only have the right to alter or abolish it, but it is also their duty and charge as free men to do so. This is not an arbitrary or populist decision, but a grave and solemn duty that must be undertaken to preserve "Safety and Happiness" for the entire nation.

— Such has been the patient sufferance of these Colonies; and such is now the necessity which constrains them to alter their former Systems of Government. The history of the present King of Great Britain is a history of repeated injuries and usurpations, all having in direct object the establishment of an absolute Tyranny over these States. To prove this, let Facts be submitted to a candid world.

It should be especially noted that the Declaration of Independence was not a secret coup or plot hatched in haste by a small group of trouble-makers. It was a formal and public "Declaration" for the entire world to witness and consider.

The Declaration of Independence was also a self-imposed death sentence to each and every man who signed his name to it. The ruling class in the parliament of Great Britain did not simply recognize the document and release the colonies from the empire. The very act of signing that historic piece of parchment was considered by the British ruling class to be an act of treason. Punishment for treason could be seizure of all property, arrest, and the execution of those responsible. Remember, in 1776 traitors were hanged, not exchanged for five terrorist leaders.

To secure for you the birthright of liberty, the original Continental Congress absolutely put their Lives, Fortunes, and Sacred Honors on the line. Should the American Revolution have failed, every man who put his name on that declaration would have been forced to surrender every earthly possession, including their lives.

How ashamed do you feel now when you complain about jury duty or say "I don't care about politics, it's all the same?" Civic duty is not a hobby or distraction, civic duty is the price for continued liberty and liberty for your children and your posterity yet unborn.

The United States of America was absolutely founded with the understanding that for the purpose of order and national security, governments needed to be formed and populated by those who had a stake in the nation. Government service was just that "service", not a career path to become a member of a self-appointed ruling class.

These are the times that try men's souls. The summer soldier and the sunshine patriot will, in this crisis, shrink from the service of their country; but he that stands by it now, deserves the love and thanks of man and woman. Tyranny, like hell, is not easily conquered; yet we have this consolation with us, that the harder the conflict, the more glorious the triumph. What we obtain too cheap, we esteem too lightly: it is dearness only that gives every thing its value.

-Thomas Paine 1776 from his work "The Crisis"

It has likely been a good while since your 10th Grade Civics class or, if you went to public school during the last twenty years, you likely glossed right over the U.S. Constitution. Let's consider the very beginning.

Preamble to the U.S. Constitution

We the people of the United States, in order to form a more perfect union, establish justice, insure domestic tranquility, provide for the common defense, promote the general welfare, and secure the blessings of liberty to ourselves and our posterity, do ordain and establish this Constitution for the United States of America.

Although generally very distrustful of sitting governments, the founding fathers understood that some form of centralized government was essential to keep the thirteen original colonies from fractioning and becoming competing independent nation states. One of the particular concerns was that the colonies/states would form independent alliances with foreign nations against the others.

The United States Constitution and the subsequent Bill of Rights were adopted not to limit the authority of the people of the country, but to limit the authority of the centralized Federal Government.

I'm hoping that all of the above is merely a refresher and that you already understand the purpose of the supreme law of the land. Sadly, far too many occupants of this nation do not. It is the sacred duty and charge of each generation to pass down to the next the lessons of the past. This duty has been largely shirked by at least the last two generations whether by choice or as the result of intellectual laziness.

Thoughts from the Founders

"Our peculiar security is in the possession of a written Constitution. Let us not make it a blank paper by construction."

Thomas Jefferson to Wilson Nicholas, 1803. ME 10:419

"They who can give up essential liberty to obtain a little temporary safety deserve neither liberty nor safety."

Benjamin Franklin's Contributions to the Conference on February 17 (III) Fri, Feb 17, 1775

"Our Constitution was made only for a moral and religious people. It is wholly inadequate to the government of any other."

John Adams, 2nd President of the United States of America

"If ye love wealth better than liberty, the tranquility of servitude than the animated contest of freedom, go from us in peace. We ask not your counsels or arms. Crouch down and lick the hands which feed you. May your chains sit lightly upon you, and may posterity forget that you were our countrymen!"

Samuel Adams, founding member of the Sons of Liberty

"...Citizens, by birth or choice, of a common country, that country has a right to concentrate your affections. The name of American, which belongs to you in your national capacity, must always exalt the just pride of patriotism more than any appellation derived from local discriminations. With slight shades of difference, you have the same religion, manners, habits, and political principles. You have in a common cause fought and triumphed together; the independence and liberty you possess are the work of joint counsels, and joint efforts of common dangers, sufferings, and successes."

George Washington from his Farewell Address upon leaving office as the 1st President of the United States

Chapter 2 Footnotes

1   "The Political Thought of the American Revolution", Clinton Rossiter, Harcourt, Brace & World, Inc. 1953

Chapter Three - Realization: Waking up Your Family and Friends

To quote George Clinton and the Funkadelic "Free your mind and your ass will follow." I am not one hundred percent certain of the method of freeing your mind that George was referencing. However, the sentiment applies to our topic of conversation. You cannot possibly hope to be a free and independent citizen if you allow yourself to be easily influenced by any manner of propaganda or media spin campaign.

The desire for freedom and an independent mind should have begun from youth. In an ideal world, young people would be taught analytical thinking from an early age. Sadly, what we know to be true is that analytical thought is not even discussed in most educational realms until college, if even then. It has been offered by some that modern colleges are not places to learn independent thought and critical or analytical thinking, just the opposite. Many so called intuitions of higher learning reward conformity and encourage 'group think'.

By the time a young person is a teenager, their way or method of thinking is largely established. The predisposition to either think independently or to accept that which is fed to the masses has been fixed long before a person might move on to secondary education. Given that the vast majority of citizens have fallen for the "if it's on TV it must be true" type of mindset, how do we combat that problem?

Personal Epiphany

It is not until a person has some kind of epiphany that they will realize the need for a change in their lives. Sadly, there are some people that you simply cannot reach. Nonetheless, it is the author's belief that more can be reached then cannot, the situation simply requires more time and effort.

How does someone have an epiphany or a striking realization? For some, this mental alarm does not go off until a traumatic event has occurred in their lives. A crisis or near-death experience may cause them to reexamine their view of the world. Sadly, many members of society do not have an epiphany until they or someone for whom they care greatly has been the victim of crime and violence or victimized by 'the system'. A prime example of this is the abysmal treatment of U.S. servicemen by the current Veteran's Administration.

It has been offered that a wise man learns from his mistakes. A wiser man learns from the mistakes of others and is determined to not allow themselves to be put into the same situation.

Reading, information gathering, and education are positive methods for learning and achieving that personal awakening. Education and learning are not necessarily interchangeable terms. It has been offered that true learning only takes place at the individual level when the person in question realizes the value and validity of the information and instruction that has previously been offered to them.

For our part here, we are going to highlight three of the most common methods used by statist or totalitarian regimes to keep the masses both subservient and disarmed. Take the time to consider each and as you move throughout your life, watch closely to see if they apply to any situation that materializes.

Ignorance

How do you convince a populace to willingly be disarmed and subservient? There are several steps and they include ignorance, distraction, and guilt.

The campaign of ignorance began decades ago with the woefully inept education system; a system that places artificial self-esteem ahead of actual achievement. The more ignorant of common law and the rights of an individual they are, the easier it becomes to dissuade the people from exercising those rights. With no understanding of history, the ignorant see the world only from the narrow view of today.

Ignorance is not stupidity. To be ignorant simply means to be without facts or knowledge. When a person is ignorant of science, mathematics, logic, reason and history, the void that is created is easily filled with emotion and artificial stimuli. When a person's head is filled with emotion they are easily manipulated.

Distraction

Distraction takes many forms. Pop-culture filth and vapid rubbish are put forth as entertainment. Rather than inspire thought and understanding, the pop culture media has devolved into baser grunts and moans.

The language is butchered and lowered to a sub-elementary level. Deviants, thugs, and reprobates are foisted as cultural icons. The impressionable generations are encouraged to be shallow and self-centered. Our culture caters to the LCD; Lowest Common Denominator. Rather that inspire and elevate, we dumb it all down.

Games and sports are promoted non-stop, keeping those who, under normal circumstances, would be outraged by the actions of the state or world events distracted. The human mind has only so much room or attention span. It is the strongly held opinion of this author that events such as "World Cup Soccer" are ideal avenues to distract the masses. World Cup Soccer is a fantastic way to distract the impoverished masses from the corruption of the state. Ditto for the NFL.

If the citizen cannot be distracted by pop culture filth, their attention is diverted to other vapid subjects. Topics of cultural dissention such as manufactured-racism, homophobia, global-warming, et al. are given non-stop publicity so as to keep the masses arguing amongst themselves and therefore distracted. Far too many citizens willfully fall into this trap.

Guilt

Finally, when the stubborn citizens, the ones who have managed, despite the odds, to educate themselves and who have turned off the cultural rot, are encountered they must be bombarded with guilt. We have borne witness to an orchestrated guilt campaign now referred to as "Fast and Furious".[1]

With absolutely no regard for the lethal consequences of their actions, those charged with protecting the lives of the innocent instead wantonly fed arms to those who they knew would use them for evil purpose. When discovered, those in charge of the fiasco claimed ignorance, good intentions, and hid behind the meaningless term "mistakes were made". Why would they do this? It is simple. The answer to the question is to force guilt upon those who stubbornly refuse to surrender their liberty of arms.

The useless horror supplied non-stop after every criminal act that includes a firearm serves the purpose of the elitist or statist. That purpose is to shame those who have escaped the ignorance and distraction traps. Guilt is a powerful ally to the ruling class elite who view the independent minded citizen as a roadblock to their conquest.

A Refuge and Fortress

The blissfully ignorant and naïve are lost. They refuse to believe, or accept, that there are those who desire to keep them uneducated, distracted, and hobbled by guilt and shame. Charles Baudelaire, not Kevin Spacey, once wrote that the greatest trick the Devil ever pulled was convincing the world he didn't exist.

If, however, you have the clarity to realize the triple threat you can, and indeed you should, gird your loins against these attacks. Educate yourself and your family in not only the law and the constitution that enumerates your God given rights, but study history. Consider the fate of all societies who willfully allowed themselves to be disarmed for the hollow promise of security.

When the seductive mistress of distraction surfaces to steal your attention away from the threats to your liberty, you must steel your mind against it. View each and every topic of discussion that is thrust upon you by the sycophant media with a jaundiced eye. Beware the trap of distraction that robs you of objectivity and entices you to turn on your fellow citizen.

Suffer not from guilt and shame. Refuse to allow the actions of the evil to persuade you to submission. How does disarming the innocent living bring back the innocent dead? Creating more potential victims through the guilt-driven disarmament does not honor the memories of those slain by armed vermin.

Genuine safety and security does not come from capitulation or surrender. It is a sad comment on our state of affairs that those who follow the aforementioned advice are so woefully in the minority.

Take hope, by all accounts it was as few as one third of the populace that led this nation through more than six years of painful revolution. The end result of their suffering was the greatest nation this world has ever known, a beacon of liberty and a shining example for all freedom loving people on Earth. The light has dimmed and it is fading, but it has not yet been extinguished. As you still draw breath you have the power to keep that fire burning. Or, as so many of your neighbors, you can simply watch "Dancing with the Stars" and let the light of liberty die out forever.

Chapter 3 Footnotes

1   Guns Across the Border, Mike Detty, SkyHorse Publishing, 2013

Never throw the first punch and Fire only if fired upon are two pieces of pseudo-tactical advice thrown out so often that people now merely parrot the phrases without ever thinking about what they mean. When examined at the most basic level the advice is often given by those who will not actually be involved in the anticipated conflict. Parents tell their kids "never throw the first punch" and Military Officers issue orders for their troops to "fire only if fired upon".

In both of the previous examples, the parent or the military officer, neither party is likely to be in actual physical jeopardy when their advice is applied. Nonetheless, telling others to exercise restraint, even to the point of putting them in harm's way, is on the face both reasonable and civilized. You see, in a perfect world where the first punch doesn't maim you and the first incoming rounds don't kill you, exercising restraint puts one on the moral high ground. Regardless of you feeling of morality, we need to consider if this strategy tactically valid or does it simply embolden and enable the aggressor?

The Shield and the Sword

"The purpose of fighting is to win. There is no possible victory in defense. The sword is more important than the shield and skill is more important than either. The final weapon is the brain. All else is supplemental."

That is one of my favorite quotes from renowned American author John Steinbeck Jr. and one I have related innumerable times during training courses.

In those few sentences, Steinbeck sums up the basic mental strategy of combat whether with a fist, a sword, or a gun. As simple and straightforward as it may seem, Mr. Steinbeck's uncomplicated advice is lost on far too many that would issue orders and or give instructions for dealing with conflict.

No soldier would go to war with only a shield in their hands. No matter how stout the shield, the enemy would eventually overwhelm it. With the shield defeated and no sword in hand, the soldier would have no options but defeat and failure.

There are those who would put all their faith in the seeking of shelter and cover from aggression or attack. Rather than go on the offensive, they take cover hoping that the attacker will eventually tire and go away. While the use of cover, from both theoretical and practical aspects is often prudent, it must be understood that all cover is temporary. A determined enemy will eventually overwhelm or circumnavigate your cover and defeat you.

We use cover as a temporary tactical device to offer protection while we strategize and prepare our attack. Hiding behind cover perpetually, as a means of avoiding the fight, is naïve and, from tactical standpoint, potentially fatal.

The thought process of today's civilized American is that defense is acceptable and moral, but anything overt, proactive, or an action that is deemed "offensive" is unacceptable, immoral, and all around "bad". Of course, this thinking flies in the face of reality.

All Cover is Temporary

When I went through Marine Corps Basic Training and then subsequently Infantry School, we were taught the meanings of cover and concealment. Concealment was simply an object or barrier that prevented the enemy from seeing or detecting you.

Cover on the other hand, was any material, barrier, structure, or object that could be relied upon to protect you from incoming small arms fire, mortars and artillery, or even bombardment. As a Marine Infantryman your first line of cover was your helmet and body armor, then simple items such as sandbags, timbers and earth.

When teaching combat with arms, whether to Marines and soldiers, police officers, or citizens, we stress the idea of being "cover conscious". We tell our students to be aware of their surroundings to the point that they can move to cover immediately if need be.

Nonetheless, we also teach that all cover is temporary. Regardless of how thick or sturdy the cover material is, eventually a determined adversary will break down that cover by continuous attack or they will maneuver around until the cover has been defeated.

In a gunfight we use cover to give us the time and opportunity to bring our weapons to bear or to formulate a strategy for victory or escape. Attempting to remain behind cover indefinitely is not a strategy or a plan; it is simply surrendering to eventual defeat.

First Punch Failure

Going back to the "never throw the first punch" advice, we are assuming that the first punch thrown is not going to knock you senseless, unconscious, break your jaw or nose. As a fighting strategy, I would NOT recommend giving Chuck Liddell (former UFC World Champion) the first punch in a fight. MMA fighters aside, neither would I recommend letting the 250-pound belligerent drunk punch you first before you decide to act. That first punch might be the last, and only, one that they need to deliver.

Do I need to remind you of the "Knock-Out Game" played by inner city vermin? This assaultive and criminal behavior encourages street thugs to practice knocking out an unsuspecting victim with a single punch. Such is the world in which we live.

The idea or advice that you should never draw your gun unless you know you are going to shoot is still floating around out there. This advice causes the person in danger to move far too slowly when dealing with a threat and also makes them pause and second guess themselves. Both of these issues can prove fatal in a fast moving violent attack.

The folly of "only fire if fired upon" is that it assumes the person(s) shooting at you is (are) incompetent or will deliberately miss you as a gesture of fair play. It only takes one single bullet to ruin your day and life.

Translated Mental Attitude

While you may never be in a position to either throw the first or second punch or return fire, the fostered mental attitude that defense is acceptable, but proactive action is wrong still pervades, even in the subconscious.

The lawful citizen, those with families and careers and reputations to uphold, will cling to the strategy of defense as their default for all matters or problems they encounter, not just physical combat. These 'civilized' and 'enlightened' people when faced with troubles and threats, rather than moving forward to deal with them, will step back and take the defensive pose. They seek cover from controversy or trouble.

The Wolves

Consider this, when our ancestors' live-stock was threatened by wolves they went out to find the wolves and killed them. They didn't bar the doors in a vain hope that the wolves would get bored and go away. They took action because action was the appropriate response.

In our modern, enlightened society, rather than band together and hunt down the wolves in a most proactive way, most of your friends and neighbors would do just the opposite. They would try to hide from the wolf. Many would go so far as to kill the weakest of their calves and leave it as an offering for the wolves thinking that they would appreciate the gift and go away. But wolves don't appreciate weakness or sacrifices. Wolves will not get bored and leave if there is prey to be had. Quite the contrary, when faced with no opposition wolves become more emboldened and vicious.

The Failure of the Defensive Mindset

While the shield is indeed a tool of defense and one that has some use, you cannot rely upon it exclusively. A professional boxer may have the best guard in the business but unless he throws a punch now and then his guard will eventually be worn down and even a mediocre fighter will defeat him. The greatest Defense in the NFL is of little use if the Offense cannot put points on the board.

The defensive strategy is merely a stopgap. A strong defense is put up to give a person time to unleash their offense. When you choose defense as your only option it becomes a recipe for eventual but certain failure. The "Defense Only" ideology puts the defender in a constant state of reaction versus action. From a completely practical standpoint, the defender, by definition, is constantly in a reactive mode and at a distinct disadvantage.

Many citizens look out at the landscape of this nation and wonder how it has come to this sad state. How is it that we are constantly losing ground in the fight of good versus evil? When faced with the pressing problems of the modern world, one can put up their shield and hide in their castle. However, given enough time, the enemy will eventually defeat the shield and breach the castle walls.

When is the time for an offensive strategy? Only you can answer that for yourself. However, first you must truly have a proactive mindset to put an offensive strategy in motion. If you, like so many others, have bought into the defense is good/offense is bad mentality, your doom and defeat are imminent.

Chapter Five - Starting the Team

During the previous chapters we have considered the "why" behind the Patriot Fire Team. Now it is time to dive into the "how". The United States Army Special Forces has a process that they refer to as "Selection". In order to become a member of the Special Forces, a soldier must successfully complete each step of Selection and there are many.

I would not dare compare the formation of local PFT with being an SF soldier, but I will offer that you should thoughtfully consider your own process of selection. For instance, if you have a friend who is fond of saying "The government needs to do something about that." they are not the person for which you are looking.

That mindset, "the government needs to do something", is a tantamount admission that they consider themselves to be helpless or at very least subservient to an all-powerful government. Such is not the mindset upon which this nation was built.

Similarly, the person who likes to tell you about each and every gun that they own should be viewed as suspect. Hear me out. If you know me, you know that I believe the cornerstone of a free people is the freedom of the citizen to possess arms.

The person who spends all of their time talking about their gun collection is either very sophomoric or they merely equate liberty to the gathering of possessions. Anyone with disposable income can buy guns. Full-fledged liberal Obama voters are gun owners too. Should those people be counted on in a time of crisis?

Naturally, anti-gun socialists who preach the collective over the individual are off the list. Perhaps they can be converted, but such a mindset is counterproductive in the arena of individual liberty. You cannot preserve a Representative Republic if you believe that human rights are handed out like candy from an all-powerful and occasionally benevolent state.

Skills and Crafts

My first choice for members of a Patriot Fire Team would be those who are successful in their careers and businesses. These folks know what it means to work hard and to make sacrifices. A small business owner whose endeavor has lasted beyond two or three years absolutely understands what it takes to make sacrifices and hard choices. No one is perfect, but the fortitude to venture out on one's own, knowing that there will be roadblocks along the way, denotes the American spirit.

If you have this text in your hands the chances are high that the idea to form a PFT will be yours. This fact makes you the de facto team leader, though you may decide to recruit someone else for that task. Regardless, someone needs to get the ball rolling and it might as well be you.

Productive communities are populated with those of varied skills. Doctors, nurses, and other medical personnel are invaluable during times of crisis. A doctor, however, may or may not be able to fix the broken radiator hose on a truck or replace the alternator. An experienced mechanic should be on the list. Carpenters, welders, and electricians all fall into the useful skills category. Community security is not just about having a gun to fend off looters.

As for approaching others to join you in this task, as daunting of a challenge at this may seem, it really need not be that scary. You may already have a group of trusted friends with whom you spend time socially. Remember, this is not some clandestine organization.

The basic question you need to honestly answer is "Upon whom would I rely to keep my family safe if I was gone and could not be there?" We aren't necessarily discussing mortality. I travel quite frequently. If I was a thousand miles away from home and a disaster occurred, whether natural or manmade, upon whom could I rely to aid my family?

If there was a major catastrophe; hurricane, massive tornado, wildfire, earthquake, with whom would I gather to ensure that our neighborhood and community was safe from looters and the scum of society that take advantage of such situations? After you have given that question considerable thought you should have your answer. If the answer is 'no one', you have quite the hill to climb.

Invite those upon whom you might rely to share an adult beverage or a cigar and pose a simple question to them. Keep your question relevant. I live on the gulf coast so annual hurricanes are always a concern. You might live in the Great White North. Ask your friends, "If we had an ice storm and the power was out for days would you be willing to help my family if I pledged to help yours?" Keeping with fragile times, you might ask "If there was widespread rioting, would you help me keep my family and home secure?" Once you have answers in the affirmative you are ready to take the next step.

Meet the Family

If they have not already been introduced, you will want to host some kind of picnic, barbecue, or gathering for all of the family members to interact socially. One of the worst things you can do is to keep your family in the dark or out of the loop. Remember, this is not some kind of secret Klan meeting.

Make it social; cook food, play baseball, pitch horseshoes, the world is grim enough without adding to the feeling of foreboding doom. No one likes to be around negative, doomsday people. We don't need defeatist communities; we need positive people. During the first gathering I would not even bring up the idea of disaster preparation. Keep it light, enjoy each other's company.

Willing and Able

It is one thing to be willing, it is entirely another to be able. If the local discount and grocery stores have been looted and burned what are you going to do about food? If someone in your group has pledged to aid you but has only a half-eaten jar of pickles and a variety condiment packets in their refrigerator they won't be much help to themselves or anyone else.

One of the biggest questions you will have to ask to all members is, "Are you prepared to be a blessing to others or a burden?" I would assume that by the fact you have gotten to this point in the text, you have the desire to be a blessing rather than a burden.

Many years ago I penned suggestions for Bronze, Silver, and Gold storm preparation plans for self-sufficiency. By self-sufficiency we mean no last minute trips to the grocery store to pick up a couple of things. Bronze is seventy-two hours, Silver is seven days and Gold is a minimum of two weeks.

After Hurricane Katrina hit the Mississippi gulf coast, there were areas that could not be reached with supply trucks for more than a week and some people did without power for an excess of three weeks. The Amish go without power twenty-four hours a day, seven days a week. How do they do it without starving to death or going crazy? Every person or family in the team needs to be willing and able to sustain their own household for at least two weeks without external support.

But Paul, you said mutual support and now you are talking about individual households. Isn't that contradictory? Not at all, by having "enough" you will likely have "more" than you need.

Say that one member of your team loses everything they own due to fire or tornado. If you have two weeks' worth of supplies could you support their family for a couple of days, or a week even, without rationing and eating the cats? Take that situation and divide it by three other members and soon you'll see that no one should have to resort to drinking out of mud puddles or rummaging through the trash cans.

If your default is to look directly to FEMA or some state emergency agency, you have entirely missed the purpose of the exercise. Despite their best efforts, state emergency agencies cannot feed the entire community even if they wanted to do so. This nation was not founded to be a nanny state where the peasants look to the king for their daily bread. Daily bread is never free and it always comes with strings attached.

I am amazed and saddened after a natural disaster to see those whose entire plan is to rely on the generosity of the state and then complain that the state is not giving them 'enough'. Even more galling are the complaints from these people that the state is not giving them what they 'want'. The ultimate exercise of the Patriot Fire Team is to foster and encourage strong, self-sufficient communities, not cities filled with desperate peasants fighting over the last loaf of bread.

Communication

During one of several instructor training courses I've taken throughout the years, the professor advised us that effective communication had three main components: sender, receiver, and message. If there is an error or problem with any of three components you cannot have effective communication.

Think about that for a moment. You may understand what you need, or the point you are trying to make, but the other party just doesn't seem to be getting it. It may be that the message needs improvement or altering. It could be that the receiver does not have the frame of reference to understand. Perhaps you could deliver the message in a different way. Possibly a phone call would be more effective than an email.

When we are discussing the team concept, communication is a key element in keeping everyone happy and working together efficiently. We have the sender, receiver, message components and then we have the mechanical delivery system.

Under normal circumstances, we communicate digitally most often; texts, emails, instant messages, etc. Actually phone calls and printed messages or instructions also work, but, what about during times of crisis?

During a weather-related emergency, electrical power and telephone communications will very likely be interrupted. During a man-made crisis; terrorist attack, riots and civil disorder, the government has granted itself the authority to limit or suspend telephone service and, yes, that means your iPhone.

Effective communication begins by everyone being on the same sheet of music or wavelength. In a sudden emergency, such as civil unrest, everyone needs to have a plan ahead of time. Family and PFT members need to have a predetermined course of action if they cannot contact each other due to telephone and/or Internet service being down. Where should family and PFT member meet or rally? Who should go where? What should you bring? All of these are questions that should be addressed before the crisis arises.

As for emergency communication hardware, handheld radios may be your first choice. There are numerous designs and models from which to choose. The FCC limits the bandwidth and signal strength. Amateur or "Ham" Radio is a source to consider. Relay systems and repeaters are in place nationwide. Keep in mind that every piece of electronic gear is going to need either an AC or a DC power source. Rechargeable batteries are nice but you need power source to regenerate them (think portable generator or car charger). Solar panels can be used to recharge small items like phone batteries.

Small battery-operated handheld radios for each team member would seem to be invaluable. You can spend anywhere from $30 up to hundreds of dollars. As with anything else, when comes to handheld radios, you get what you pay for.

Let's get into the 'daily bread' discussion in detail. As highlighted during a previous chapter, you cannot eat your ammo. There are those who delude themselves into believing that if things ever get "too bad", they will simply hunt and kill what they need to eat. Even if you are a hunter, ask yourself this, when is the last time you fed your entire family for a week with wild game you killed, processed, and prepared one hundred percent with your own hands?

If you live in an urban or suburban area, are you willing to bet your family's lives on the chance that you can kill enough deer, rabbits, squirrels, etc. to feed them all for three days, seven days, or two weeks? How are you going to keep your family secure from the threat of looting, rape, and robbery if you are out hunting for wild game? If you live on a 5000 acre ranch I suppose you can be excused from this exercise, but the vast majority of America does not.

BRONZE PLAN: 72 hours of self-sufficiency

We are talking about a full 72 hours without any outside assistance. You must have the food, clean drinking water, meds, fuel, batteries for flashlights etc. to sustain you and your family for a minimum of 72 hours. You cannot rely on outside utilities; electric, gas, city water, etc. Don't plan on having telephone service or the time to run out for last minute items.

When it comes to food, I like to have a three pronged attack; canned food that requires no refrigeration, dehydrated food that can be prepared by simply adding cold or boiling water, and bulk food items such as rice, corn, flour, sugar, honey, etc. Jerky and other dried meats fall somewhere in the middle. Drinking water should be stored as individual bottles, gallon jugs and large bulk containers.

Don't forget hygiene. You still need to use the toilet and keep yourself clean. Washing your hands is important, even if the electricity is out. Think of the situation as if you are deep woods camping. All you have is what you brought with you.

SILVER PLAN: 7 Days of self-sufficiency

Have enough food, water, supplies to support your family for seven days without external assistance. Long term water storage can be accomplished by simply putting tap water into sealable containers. Use household chlorine bleach to treat water and prevent bacteria: 1/2 teaspoon of bleach for 10 gallons of water and 2 teaspoons for 50 gallons.

Bulk food is great but it can be bland. Remember to have spices on hand. Eating plain white rice three times a day will get old quickly. My personal go-to hot sauce is "Texas Pete". A quart of hot sauce is only a few dollars. Salt and pepper will keep nearly forever if stored properly. A keg of salt is around a buck at the grocery store, less if they are on sale.

Household chlorine bleach is cheap and should always be kept on hand for cleaning and water treatment. Any area that will be used for food preparation should be cleaned and sanitized regularly. Ditto for white vinegar, keep as least a gallon on hand.

Proper hygiene is critically important when "the lights go out". Living through a natural disaster is tough enough without being sick. Hand sanitizer helps to save valuable, freshwater. How much TP do you have on hand? Consider purchasing a package of moist, disposable hand towels and putting them in your emergency cabinet.

After several days you are going to need to do laundry. Are you equipped to do laundry without electricity? Do you own something as simple as a clothes line with pins? The local Dollar Store should have clothes line and clothespins for a few bucks.

Do you have the means to burn trash; a burn barrel or fire pit? Mounds of trash will attract rodents, vermin, and flies that carry disease and bacteria. Do you own common hand tools: spade shovel, flat shovel, steel garden rake, etc.? You will need them.

GOLD PLAN: Two weeks' plus

Hopefully by this point you have stocked at very least 72 hours' worth of food, water, meds, etc. If not, why not? As we progress up the ladder of self-sufficiency we will consider what we will dub the "Gold Plan". The Gold Plan is two weeks, 14 full days of self-sustainment. The same rules apply as before. You cannot rely on external assistance from FEMA or some state agency.

The Gold Plan can also be thought of as the Katrina plan. During the aftermath of Hurricane Katrina there were people who lived for several weeks without electricity. It also took many weeks to clear all of the roadways; interstates were first, then state highways, then the county roads. Many bridges were destroyed and roads washed out and impassible. Even when trucks with supplies were dispatched it was difficult to reach many parts of the gulf coast.

For the Gold Plan to work you need to do some calculating. Determine how many people you will be feeding and calculate the number of meals. You can survive on two meals a day or, better yet, spread out small meals during the day. Regarding drinking water, it is recommended that you have one gallon per person per day. A family of five for two weeks equals 70 gallons of water. Bulk water storage will be more convenient and practical than 70 one-gallon water jugs stacked up on shelves.

Consider a water reservoir or catch system. Rainwater can be treated to drink in a pinch and also used for non-potable tasks. You might be amazed at how much water you go through in a day without realizing it. Strongly suggested are water-purification filter pitchers from discount stores. Remember to buy extra filters.

Prescription medicine and vital items like insulin can be the difference between life and death. Do you keep critical medications on hand? Could you survive for two weeks without a trip to the pharmacy? These are tough questions but times can be tough. Start your storm preparation yesterday.

Forever Food

There are certain foods or, more appropriately, food staples that, if stored properly, can literally outlive you. The list can easily be found online, but here are some for your consideration.

Honey, Rice, Sugar, Hard Liquor, Maple Syrup, Pure Vanilla Extract, Distilled White Vinegar, Cornstarch, and Salt are all food staple items that will last for decades if stored properly. Flour, dried corn and dried beans naturally will last a very long time as well.

The key to longevity for any type of stored food is to keep the moisture and bugs out of it. It should go without saying that the ubiquitous "cool, dry, away from direct sunlight" storage advice should be followed for long term storage food items.

Chapter Seven - The Patriot Arsenal

If you are an American citizen living in a free state, your choices in the firearms category are vast. It is easy to get lost in a sea of confusion when the time comes to choose. Quite frankly, most men have a tendency to 'over-think' the issue and make the decision more difficult than it truly needs to be.

When pressed to pick a "Top 3" for defensive firearms, the choice is not all that difficult but it does indeed require a bit of analytic thought. What I will detail in the following paragraphs are not simply my personal choices for a Patriot Arsenal, but I will detail the reasons behind my thinking. These thoughts are based upon three decades of carrying a firearm for a living and teaching others to employ said arms.

M4/AR Rifle

The first component to the Patriot Arsenal is some type of AR or M4 style rifle or carbine based upon the original Gene Stoner design. Despite the wide variety of chambering available, I would initially stick with a rifle/carbine that is a true 5.56mm. Regardless of regional or anecdotal evidence to the contrary, .223 Remington or 5.56mm is still the most commonly available cartridge for this style of long gun. Until the United States Military changes to another caliber, the aforementioned fact will remain true. Love it or hate it, every ammunition manufacturer in the United States puts a great deal of time and effort into building the .223 Remington cartridge.

As for firearm parts, components, and accessories, again, there are more of all of these available for the standard AR rifle than any other rifle in production today. To that end, the modern AR has become the "Mr. Potato Head" of the gun world. There are innumerable configurations and modifications that can be made to the base gun without detailed custom work or the requirement to ship the gun back to the manufacture or a gunsmith. AR rifle owners can swap out the original upper receiver for one of a different caliber or change out the stock, grips, and forends without much trouble, should they choose to do so later on.

When it comes to practical use, the AR chambered in .223/5.56mm is a top contender for personal defense work in and around the home. Modern ammunition in this configuration is better than it ever has been. Ammunition with bullet weights in the 55 to 77 grain range are excellent for self-defense work and up to the job of taking small to medium sized predators and game. For instance, the 77 grain Mk262 load from Black Hills Ammunition is not only doing yeoman's work on the enemies of this nation overseas, it is also up to the challenge of taking wild game in excess of two hundred pounds.

An aspect of the AR or M4 that cannot be overlooked is the relative ease of operation once the shooter has been trained, and the relatively mild recoil it produces for a centerfire rifle. Any physically fit adult, regardless of age, size, or sex should be able to use the AR effectively. This is critically important, as all of the responsible adults in the household should be able to use the self-defense guns, not just the strongest and most experienced shooter.

AR or M4 style guns with flat-top upper receivers allow the end user to install a variety of sight configurations and optics. Standard iron sights, 1 to 1 (non-magnified) red dot optics, and magnified rifle scopes can all be fitted to the guns with relative ease.

Pump Action Shotgun

The next gun on the list is the pump action shotgun chambered in 12 gauge. Yes, there are a number of semi-automatic guns available of high quality, but their operation tends to be a bit more complex and many have a tendency to be particular when it comes to ammunition. A 20 gauge gun does indeed produce less recoil, but the variety of ammunition available for the 12 gauge eclipses all others.

A pump action shotgun is not a perfect tool, but it is a tool that adds depth and breadth to the self-defense arsenal. For lethal force encounters against predators, both two and four-legged, some type of buckshot load or single projectile slug is most effective. For nuisance animals or venomous threats, some type of birdshot load should be practical. There are specialty munitions for 12 gauge, such as audible and visual emergency signaling rounds, that, while a bit expensive, may be useful to the patriot.

Like the AR, the operation of the pump action shotgun is a relatively straight-forward matter and a novice shooter can be taught to use it in a comparatively short time. While felt recoil is more considerable than an AR rifle chambered in .223 Remington, the shotgun does indeed fill a role that is difficult for a centerfire carbine match.

Striker-Fired Pistol

We have deliberately saved the handgun section for last as it is an area that will predictably be met with the most contention and confusion. Depending on the knowledge and practical experience of the shooter, choices will vary greatly. It is a bit ironic that when it comes to genuine self-protection, from the standpoints of physics or ballistics, the handgun is the least effective fight stopper of the three types of firearms mentioned, but the most contentious. Handgun choice is more greatly influenced by the male ego than any other firearm decision.

In the American gun market there are quite literally thousands of handguns from which to choose. To make the most practical purchase we need to consider for what purpose the firearm will be used. In our discussion here, we are looking for firearms that have a relatively short learning curve, are reliable, and have readily available accessories and ammunition. Holster availability and spare magazines are also big on the list.

Given the previous criteria, I would absolutely recommend one of several types of striker-fired pistols currently available from major manufacturers. The Smith&Wesson M&P9 is top of the list. That pistol comes in a variety of sizes; full, compact, and sub-compact (Shield). On the M&P9, the grip/backstrap can be quickly swapped from small to medium to large without tools or a gunsmith. From personal experience, the S&W M&P9 is infinitely reliable and accurate. Thanks to American law enforcement embracing these guns, numerous holster designs can be readily had, as well as spare magazines.

Other striker-fired pistols of note would include the Springfield-Armory XD(M), the Ruger SR9, and the GLOCK 19 or 17. In the spare magazine and accessory department, the 9mm GLOCK pistols take the prize. Of late, the TP9SA and SF pistols from Century Arms have come on strong as a top contender. They are inexpensive and the author has had tremendous success with them.

All of the aforementioned guns function in a similar fashion. If you can run one of them, you can run them all. The 9x19mm chambering is my preference. A pistol will NEVER be as potent as a rifle or shotgun regardless of caliber. Modern defensive ammunition for the 9mm cartridge is quite good and 9mm practice ammunition is the most cost-effective load of any centerfire pistol as these words are written.

M&P9 pistol has a seventeen round magazine. If my wife or teenaged children ever had to defend themselves with a handgun, I'd rather they had rounds left over when the fight was finished than to be in the middle of the fight and run out. Also, wives and teenagers can easily be taught to manage the felt recoil from the 9mm, while the .40S&W can be quite brutal and the frame size of many .45ACP guns can be a bit wide for small to medium hands.

I am guessing that you have by now noticed the glaring omission of .22 Long Rifle (rimfire) long guns and handgun. The purpose was not to slight the many quality models available. If we were making a list of "bug out" or "survivalist" guns a .22LR would definitely make the cut, but our purpose here is personal defense first and utility second.

Assembling the Arsenal

Your personal experience, bias, or preference may lead you in a different direction than the one I've outlined herein, but at very least you will have some place to start. Most importantly, you have food for thought as to which type of hardware may or may not be appropriate for you own Patriot Arsenal.

Arsenal On a Budget

If you have been running the numbers through your mental calculator, you likely have come up with a figure in the $2000 neighborhood to complete a Patriot Arsenal as I have described it. That amount does not take into account a quality optic for the AR. Fear not, for those of you with sticker shock, I have come up with an "on a budget" patriot arsenal that should be within reach of every person with a regular income.

Mosin-Nagant

While you may have your heart set on a tricked-out AR, reality may dictate that the thousand dollars or so it would cost is out of the question. Remember you are assembling a kit of firearms, not a single unit.

The Mosin-Nagant rifles and carbines in their numerous configurations are not only stout and robust fighting guns; they are priced right, even in today's market. The 7.62x54R (rimmed) cartridge is the most economical .30 caliber centerfire rifle round available. Think of the 7.62x54R as the Russian version of the .30-06 Springfield. A solid hit with a .30 caliber bullet from a Nagant rifle will get the immediate attention of any predator. If you doubt the value, price a box of twenty .30-06 cartridges with a comparable box of 7.62x54R.

Yes, these rifles are large and they come with steel buttplates. They do, however, handle very well and point quite naturally. The Nagant bolt-action is one of the top designs in world military history, second possibly to the Mauser action and the Enfield.

Certainly there are numerous options available to the American gun buyer. The Mosin-Nagant has the advantage of low cost in the rifle itself, low cost for ammunition, a stellar reputation for reliability and it offers enough ballistic firepower to get the job done.

Fringe benefits include a hardwood stock, steel buttplate, and most models today come with an eighteen-inch bayonet. Do not be so quick to dismiss the bayonet as an antique. Would you try to bully your way past a man holding a four-foot-long rifle with a foot and a half long bayonet on the business end? Similarly, would the leader of a group of looters and thugs put his mob up against four men confidently holding the aforementioned rifles? The Mosin-Nagant rifles do not seem so much like quaint antiques and wall-hangers now, do they?

Keeping with our budget shopping endeavor, the pump-action 12 Gauge shotgun is still within easy reach. You might have to forego a Picatinny rail and pistol grip. The Mossberg 500 or near identical Maverick guns can be had in the $200 range.

Regarding striker-fired 9mm pistol, there are several units available in the $350 to $450 range. Century Arms is a purveyor of several inexpensive pistol models. As these words go to print the Canik TP9SA and SF 9x19mm pistols are retail priced around $350.

Ammunition

I suppose that no chapter on firearms would be complete without a discussion of ammunition. It is my sincere hope that the great Ammo Crisis of 2012/2013 taught us all a valuable lesson. And yes, I realize many of you in "the choir" were never affected because you had prepared.

A car without gasoline is essentially a giant flower pot. A gun without ammunition is an expensive club. How much is enough? Only you can decide that for yourself. Personally I would not feel comfortable without a thousand rounds of FMJ practice ammunition for my chosen firearms and one hundred rounds of more expensive, higher quality ammunition designed for personal defense. Yes, there absolutely is a difference.

Practice Ammunition

Practice or target ammunition is purpose built to be less expensive. In today's world there is no such thing as 'cheap' ammunition but there is ammunition that is more 'cost effective'. Training or practice ammunition is purposely built with less expensive components. By using less expensive components the manufacturer is able to reduce the consumer cost, thus allowing you to shoot more for less money. Practice ammunition will be loaded with full metal jacket (non-expanding) or solid lead bullets and the cases will be standard brass, lacquered steel, or aluminum.

One of the 'less expensive components' put into practice ammunition is the propellant powder. Yes, there is a difference in powders and some are costlier than others. The powder in practice ammo is generally, but not always, a bit dirtier. That is, it tends to produce that gray smoke cloud and leaves behind considerably more carbon on the gun. Practice ammo also has a tendency to produce a very bright flash.

Fighting Ammunition

When a manufacturer produces a fighting load, one that the shooter will be using to protect their life, they use premium or more expensive components. A quality defensive load will have a controlled expansion bullet. These come in many varieties but all are designed to expand/open up when they strike something solid like animal tissue. The reason for this is two-fold; expanding bullets reduce the chance of the bullet passing completely through the target and they also will potentially do more damage to the target thus reducing the number of rounds it takes to neutralize the threat.

Some of the premium components include nickel (silver) cases, sealed (moisture-proof) primers, and flash-reducing propellant powder. Because defensive ammunition is built from premium components it is naturally more expensive. In this case, you get what you pay for. It is expected that fighting ammunition will spend a considerable amount of time loaded in the gun, in 'stand-by' mode for that just in case moment. In such a case it may be wise to spend that little bit extra.

Bonus Material

Thoughts about Body Armor: Paranoid or Prepared?

It's hard enough convincing citizens that it is indeed a valid idea to carry a concealed firearm for personal protection against unforeseen threats. Mention the use of body armor and the wailing truly begins. "A bullet-proof vest, just how paranoid are you?" was one statement I heard. "I don't ever plan to be in a position where I'd need body armor." was another.

Yes, it is true that unless you are in a profession that requires you to move toward the sound of gunfire, you don't ever "plan" to be in a gunfight. Nonetheless, the choice is rarely up to you. I don't plan to be in a car crash but I still carry automobile insurance and I wear my seat belt.

Armor Sucks

If you are one of the tens of thousands of citizens who owns and carries a firearm for personal protection you've likely accepted the fact that bad things can, and do, happen to good people. You've adjusted your manner of dress and lifestyle to accommodate toting your chosen type of hardware. Carrying a gun every day definitely takes some adjustment.

As someone who has worn armor, both concealed and external for over twenty-five years I can tell you one thing: wearing armor sucks. Armor makes you sweat, even in cold weather, it's heavy and constantly rubs you the wrong way. Granted, it doesn't suck as bad as it did when I was a USMC Private or a rookie police officer. Armor technology and carriers have definitely improved over the last couple of decades.

Comfort, however, is relative. When I was with the 6th Marines laying in shallow ditch with artillery shells screaming overhead and incoming mortars exploding far too closely, my flak jacket and helmet were pretty darn comforting. Later in life, while searching a darkened building for possible suspects, I felt a bit more comfort in knowing that my Level IIIA armor vest with a hard plate covering my heart was under my polyester uniform shirt. Armor, like insurance or your gun, is an item that you are glad to have "just in case" things don't go your way.

Paranoid or Prepared?

I can think of myriad reasons why a citizen might want the extra bit of comfort that soft body armor provides. Any merchant who deals in cash or valuables like gold or jewelry is, by profession, in a precarious occupation. A home invasion where the police are fifteen minutes away and the gang-bangers at your front door are seconds away is another. We also have the ugly but very realistic scenarios of civil unrest after a storm, during a riot, etc.

We can't always predict what tomorrow might bring. It's easy to talk yourself out of being prepared to face evil because evil isn't always in your face. However, evil is always present, like it or not.

Choices: Hard vs. Soft

First of all, there is no such thing as a "bullet-proof" vest. For every type and style of armor available, there is a projectile that will penetrate it. However, there are multiple levels or layers of bullet-resistant armor. I have no inclination to get into the National Institute of Justice "Level" rating for armor, as that would only confuse the matter.

What's more important is to discuss what armor is available to you. When it comes to wearable armor you have hard and soft as well as concealable and external. Soft body armor is generally a panel of some shape made from a pliable, flexible material. DuPont's Kevlar® is the most commonly used material, though there are others.

Hard armor takes the form of inflexible plates, again, made in various shapes and sizes. The material used to make hard armor plates varies from hardened steel covered in nylon or rubber to some type of hardened/reinforced ceramic.

Soft armor is relatively light and, because it is flexible, can be wrapped around a human torso.

Hard armor is strategically placed over the front and back of the torso to shield vital organs.

The rub is that soft armor is only capable of stopping low velocity projectiles to include handgun bullets, shotgun pellets, and fragmentation from explosions. Hard armor is capable of stopping all the aforementioned threats, but it can also defeat high velocity projectiles from rifles and shotgun slugs. Yes, there are projectiles with steel/tungsten cores that will penetrate hard armor, but let's stick to the basics here.

Concealable or External

Both hard and soft armor can be concealed or worn in covert or external carriers. The benefit of concealable armor, naturally, is that it doesn't stand out or draw attention to the wearer. The downside is that is requires some effort to don and can be less than comfortable.

External armor carriers, for both hard and soft armor, are obvious but also far more utilitarian. Overt carriers can be outfitted with a variety of pouches to tote myriad gear including spare ammunition, medical gear, a handgun, phone or radio, etc. Overt armor carriers generally are easy to don and can be put on quickly in an emergency.

Which armor carry method is the best? It depends on your circumstance. A gold dealer walking around in the city would naturally be better served by a concealed vest. The homeowner who wants armor they can throw over their body in an emergency isn't worried about being discreet.

Legality

Is it legal for every citizen in every state to own body armor? Probably not. Just as gun ownership and concealed carry laws vary from state to state, so do regulations regarding personally owned armor.

If you live in a state that restricts your 2nd Amendment rights, you can feel confident that the elitists in your State House have seen fit to restrict your ability to save your own life with soft body armor. Ultimately the responsibility rests with you. If you are unsure, do your own research.

*As these words are printed, there is currently a move underway in the U.S. House of Representative to make it a felony nationwide to possess certain types of body armor.

How valuable is your life?

Much of the push-back from our side of the aisle when it comes to citizen ownership of soft body armor stems from the "reasonableness disease". I've been a party to conversations with gun owners where the topic of body armor came up. One person opined, "Civilians don't need that (armor), it's best left for police and the military. I mean, how paranoid are you?"

That statement says that the speaker believes three (3) things: 1) the life of someone in a uniform is more valuable than that of a citizen 2) working for a government agency bestows special rights not afforded to the citizenry 3) the person making the statement has no understanding of what a violent assault entails.

The first two of these assertions should be troubling to every freedom loving American citizen.

Sadly, far too many people that should be our allies have been fooled into believing that the life of the 'average citizen' is somehow worth less than that of someone in uniform. They accept that 'civilians' should not be 'allowed' to own body armor.

While preparing this review I read a story of a home owner in Pontiac, Michigan defending his pregnant wife and child from multiple felons. The online newspaper reported that sometime after 3 a.m. on the day in question two armed home invaders broke into the family's house. The husband/father exchanged gunfire with the vermin and they fled.

One of the felons was wounded and arrested later at a local hospital. Three men have been charged in the crime; there was a getaway driver. However, the homeowner died as a result of the gunshot wounds he received in the attack, his wife along with both children, born and unborn, escaped unharmed.

Could civilian body armor have saved his life? Would the man have had time to put it on? Perhaps, but in this case we'll never know. This leads me to an important question. What is more important in a gunfight; shooting the bad guy or not getting shot? The answer is: not getting shot. Remember, you can win your gunfight but still die. The whole point of personal defense is to win the gunfight and stay alive.

Self-trained shooters are much like self-taught motorcycle riders. As long as they go slow and never encounter any kind of obstacle, or the unexpected, they can operate within acceptable safety margins. However, if they face an unforeseen challenge, get nervous or are forced by circumstance to go faster than normal, both of the aforementioned people are an accident waiting to happen.

Can you imagine a medical student arguing that they should not be required to intern because they passed their anatomy class? Similarly, I drive my car back and forth to work each day, surely I could qualify for a NASCAR event next weekend. No, the aforementioned are ridiculous assertions, but that is the kind of thinking we get from gun owners.

Folks, when it comes to engaging in the "gravest extreme", as my friend Massad Ayoob once put it, knowing how to load a gun and press the trigger is not what I would call training. Dealing with a deadly force attack is the highest level of stress you will ever encounter. You owe it to yourself to have more than scant knowledge of how a gun works.

I have always found it puzzling that for many men admitting that they are not 'experts' with a firearm is somehow tantamount to confessing impotence. We are not born good shooters. However, the male portion of society, for some strange reason, has an innate belief that possession of testicles de facto makes them skilled drivers, lovers, and shooters.

The hierarchy of combat readiness from most important to least is: Mindset, Tactics, Skill and Gear. American men often fall into the trap of believing that purchasing gear makes up for deficiencies on the other three categories or that gear purchase bestows skill.

Before we get too deep into the weeds, let us consider the difference between practice and training. For our discussion herein those two words are not necessarily interchangeable. Training is something you do under the watchful eye and tutelage of an experienced instructor. Practice is used for skill maintenance. My good friend James Yeager likes to say that "Training teaches you what and how to practice." We take training at a school so we can return home and practice what we have been taught.

One of the greatest intangibles that you get from training is confidence. We are talking about genuine confidence that is a product of education and achievement, not the bull-crap false confidence passed out like candy in our public schools. The "you're okay, I'm okay" and "everyone gets a trophy for showing up" social babble garbage does nothing but provide false security and fake confidence.

Genuine confidence is as valuable as gold and just as difficult to acquire. Confidence comes from the formation of skill. Another instructor friend of mine once stated that education combined with dedicated practice results in skill. You don't get skill from sitting in a classroom watching a PowerPoint presentation. Similarly, you cannot appreciate the value of practice if you do not understand the purpose of the exercise.

Books and video material offer education and stimulate thought. These methods of delivery can also provide a motivation to seek out training. Of the most difficult steps in training, understanding or coming to the realization that you actually need to take the training is one of the hardest and most important stages of learning.

Just like an alcoholic cannot get help until they realize they have a problem, a student cannot begin the learning process until they admit that they do not already know it all. In order to grow you must accept that you are a beginner once, but you are a student for life. The best instructors I know are constantly seeking out education and information. These men do not sit back and say "I'm an instructor now. I don't need any more training."

When I conduct a Pistol 101 beginner's course I regularly remind students that the intro program is not the end of their training life, but the beginning. For thirty years now I've been a dedicated student of the gun. If you want to impress your instructor, don't tell them about how many guns you own, tell them how many training certificates you have earned.

It is not until you go out and get professional training that you realize how much you don't know. If you are intellectually honest with yourself, you may very likely leave your first class with more questions about mindset, tactics and skill than you had when you arrived. That is a positive thing.

We have all heard the "turkeys and eagles" analogy; you cannot soar with the eagles if you flock with the turkeys. When the topic of training comes up you will hear much pseudo-advice from the turkeys. There are those who will ask why you would want to train; after all you are 'pretty good'. The underachievers will spout ridiculous statements such as "I know how to shoot a gun. You just point it and pull the trigger."

Get away from those people. They wish to drag you down into their "C- "world. They have either given up on trying to achieve any type of goal or they are so comfortable in their own mediocrity that they feel threatened by someone who desires more. These people have already given up and they want you to join them in their 'good enough' world.

Based simply upon the fact that you have this text in your hands, I will assume that you have the desire to be more than a C- student. Now that we have discussed the reasons for taking training as an individual, let's consider training for the team.

Team Training

The foundation of any team is the common goal and common experiences. United States Military Special Operations Units function at the highest level largely due to the fact every member of the unit has had to go through the same selection process. These men have all slept in the mud, hiked and humped until they thought they would pass out. They have run until they thought they would puke, then puked, then kept on running. Operators start with basic training, and then go to infantry school, advanced infantry school, and innumerable technical and specialty schools.

By the time they are assembled together as a team, the aforementioned men have a common set of skills and goals. Having done such, the team members mesh and function not as a gaggle of individuals, but a cohesive unit.

As for the Patriot Fire Team, I would strongly suggest that every member have attended, at very least, a two-day fighting pistol course from a reputable training academy. That is the beginning, not the end.

It would naturally be ideal for PFT members to all take the same course at the same time. This could be a pistol, shotgun, or carbine course.

Even though the course may be tailored to individual shooters, the fact that everyone on the team has the same experience and basic skill set will go a long way to establishing a cohesive team mindset.

Logically, the next step is to attend a course that focuses specifically on partner tactics or team building. It is exceptionally rare to find a small unit training course in the private sector, but "partner" classes can be found. Fighting Rifle from Tactical Response introduces shooters to two-man tactics.

Remember, training teaches you what and how to practice. If your team members have a common training background they will understand what and how to practice at the home range.

Safety and Risk

It cannot be stressed highly enough that safety on the training range is best achieved when everyone is competent and experienced. Live-fire training is a dangerous undertaking and it involves risk. That fact does not mean we should not undertake the endeavor; it simply means we need to take educated steps to mitigate risk.

Every man or woman on the range is a safety officer and has the authority of point out safety risks and violations of the 4 Universal Safety Rules. Park your ego. The more time we spend around firearms, the more comfortable we become with them and the higher the risk for negligence.

Universal Safety Rules:

Keep your finger straight and off the trigger until the sights are aligned and you've made the decision to fire. This is the number one most broken safety rule. Remember, "Off target, off trigger". The trigger is not a finger rest. *When not engaged in firing, the trigger finger must be up along the slide or receiver.

Treat All Guns as if they are loaded all the time. A firearm can only be considered unloaded after it has been verified by two independent means. This could be two people checking the gun or one person inspecting the gun both visually and physically.

Never allow the muzzle to cover anything you are not willing to destroy. Before you point a firearm at anything ask yourself "If the gun fires, will anything bleed?"

Know your target, what is around it and what is beyond it. Not every round will strike the center of your intended target and many of those that do will pass through the target and continue to travel. Remember you own every round that exits your firearm.

Fighting and First Aid

While skill with arms is an absolute must for all men who would aspire to freedom and liberty, there is much more to the equation. Not every problem you encounter will be a shooting problem.

Each and every team member should have a fundamental understanding of traumatic medical care. Taking a fighting first aid course, such as Beyond the Band Aid, is yet another excellent opportunity for team members to bond and build cohesion.

One of the biggest fallacies that modern Americans have is that they have the Constitutional Right to defend their lives with a gun, but somehow they have no right to stop gap a major bleeding injury. If you have the mentality that you could take a life in the gravest extreme, why would you not save the life of someone you love or care about in the same circumstance?

A non-shooting class, such as basic land navigation (also known as orienteering) once again offers the opportunity for team building and is not so much "life and death" as other fighting classes.

Do you really want to see how team members will react under stress? Get everyone together for a day or weekend of horseback riding. If you've never been on the back of thousand-pound animal, it can be quite the humbling experience.

A word of caution: until everyone on the team is comfortable with each other's skills and has a mutual respect for the common goal, I recommend against self-taught or self-guided training. There is an absolute Alpha Male undertone going on, and that is quite natural. However, for the first couple of team building events, let someone else be the Alpha Male. Let the instructor be the Alpha while the team members learn and develop skill. Nothing will kill a team faster that unchecked and misguided ego clashes.

Getting Ready for Shooting School

We all love to buy guns and gear. However, buying gear does not impart the ability to use it effectively. All responsible American gun owners should, at some point in time, take the opportunity to attend professional training.

If you have booked a seat in a shooting school you've likely already decided what gun and which holster you are going to take. Our desire in the next several paragraphs will be to discuss numerous items that you might not have considered.

Planning a trip to a shooting school is a big deal. You block out the time and cash in some vacation days. From a monetary standpoint you have to factor the price of tuition, travel, lodging and meals. Don't forget to consider the ammunition cost.

With all these things in mind you want to make sure that you are getting the most out of your experience. Showing up without the proper gear, poorly made gear and/or no foul weather clothing is a recipe for disaster.

Regarding gear and how much you should spend, shooting gear is no different than anything else you might purchase for your home or car. If you shop around you can indeed find discounts and sales on certain items, but cheap gear is always cheap gear.

Would you put $10 tires on your car even if you could find them? How long would you expect $10 tires to last? Gun people will purchase the cheapest holster they can find and then act surprised or offended when it breaks on the range.

The model for gear purchases is to buy the best gear you can afford. Paying $1000 for a pistol and then sticking it in a $19 holster does not make any sense. Maybe you would be better served by an $800 pistol with the remaining money going toward a quality holster, magazines, and training ammunition?

Head to Toe

It doesn't matter how tough you perceive yourself to be, if you are cold, wet, and have sore feet, your attention isn't going to be on learning. Starting from the ground up, ensure you have comfortable, well-fitting boots or shoes. Better yet, pack out two comfortable, well-made sets of footwear that you can use on the range.

All training schools that I'm aware of operate rain or shine. Unless there is severe weather and lightning, you can expect to do outside training. If your boots get soaked the first day, they aren't likely to be dry by the next morning when you need them. Believe me. You don't want to start the day off putting your feet into wet boots.

Along the same line, pack quality socks. Pack one or two more pairs than you think you'll need. They weigh next to nothing but are invaluable if you need them. Ditto for T-shirts.

Regarding weather, take the time to research the average temperature and weather forecast for the area where you will be traveling. Think layers. Cold mornings in the high desert give way quickly to hot afternoons. Conversely, a sunny morning in the Midwest can easily become a rainy afternoon. You'll never regret taking a quality rain jacket with an insulated liner. However, it's easy to regret forgetting to do so or going 'cheap'. A $2.00 rain poncho will be ripped and torn after your first drill.

As far as normal classroom and range wear, long pants and long sleeve shirts are the way to go. There is going to be brass flying and that stuff is hot when it lands on bare skin, particularly rifle brass. Knee pads are another investment you will appreciate if your class is more dynamic than simple marksmanship training. To steal another quote from my friend James, "Kneepads are cheaper than new knees."

Read the List

I know most men are visual, hands-on learners and they don't ask for directions but, do yourself a favor, read the recommended gear list. Most every school has a detailed, recommended gear list. They do this for a living, take their advice. The school knows what you should bring.

Regarding the style of holster, it is very important to follow the school's guidelines. Most professional shooting academies do not allow shoulder holsters and cross-draw rigs on their ranges. If the school recommends that you bring at least three magazines for your pistol, don't try to short cut them and bring one or two. There is a method to their madness. Stuff breaks, you are better off to have extra than not enough.

Regarding gear, especially magazines, take the time to mark it all before you go to the school. Every GLOCK 17 or Beretta M9 magazine looks like every other one. Sharpie markers and paint pens from the craft section are fantastic for marking your gear. Trust me, at some point in time you'll drop, misplace or forget a piece of gear. If your name is on it, chances are good you will get it back.

It should go without saying, ensure you have the correct safety gear. Wrap-around shooting glasses and protective muffs. If you have the means, spend the extra money for electronic hearing protection. These cut down on some of the frustration from not being able to hear the teacher and having to constantly take the muffs off to listen to instruction.

Physical Fitness

Few privately run shooting courses will rival the Marine Recon Indoctrination, nonetheless, expect to exert some physical effort. At very least, you'll be spending a lot of time on your feet. If you have a genuine physical infirmity your instructors will work with you, but soft and out of shape is not a legitimate handicap.

You should have plenty of lead time before the course. If you haven't gotten any exercise lately, this might be good time to start. Remember, you are investing in yourself. You are not taking training for the instructors or your peers. I'm not telling you to prep for a marathon, but you should be able to make it to lunch without a nap.

Attitude

I have deliberately saved this subject for last, not because it is of least importance, it's just the opposite. Regardless of the guns and gear you are equipped with; your attitude is the most critical factor in determining how much you will get out of a training course.

Park your ego. You are not going to the school to impress the instructors with how much you think you already know. Mouth closed, ears wide open is the best advice I can give. Take a notebook and a pen with you to record copious notes and don't be afraid to ask pertinent questions or to seek clarification.

Because of the constraints of time, the instructors must put out a great deal of material during a relatively short time span. You will never regret taking plenty of notes so you can refer back to them once you've returned home.

Parting Thoughts

For those outside the of the military or law enforcement realm, planning a trip to a professional firearms academy is a bit of an adventure. You are getting out of your 'pond' and leaving your personal comfort zone, and that is a good thing. It's nearly impossible to grow or improve in any area of endeavor without professional guidance, or at least honest peer critique.

The best firearms instructors in the nation are those that constantly travel to schools other than their own. Retired Master Sergeant Paul

Howe, who owns CSAT, a school in Texas, recently wrote, "Training, like selection, is a never ending process. We begin learning on day one of our life."

Whether you are planning a weekend or a week at a professional training course, you will be well served to take the time to prepare your mind, body, and kit bag. Never kid yourself by thinking "I'll just pick up 'x' when I get there." Referring back to my Marine Corps days, you should be ready to go as soon as your boots hit the ground.

Chapter 9 - Defeating Terrorists in the 21st Century

As an American Patriot and citizen you must understand that the greatest external threat to the safety and stability of the United States of America in the 21st Century is radical Islam, and any self-proclaimed Muslim that does not publicly denounce these terrorists. To remain silent is to offer acceptance. There is no room in this fight for moderates or fence-sitters.

For those who went to public school during the last twenty years or who have a short memory, we will take a moment to consider the history of terrorism in the 20th Century, and the methods that were employed to defeat it. Yes, it was defeated, not negotiated with.

The People's Armies

Action Directe, the Red Brigades, the Baader-Meinhof Gang (also known as the Red Army Faction), November 17, and the Japanese Red Army, these Communist/Marxist terrorist organizations were in the papers and on the evening news weekly, if not a daily basis, during the seventies and eighties. Bombings, kidnappings, and assassinations were their modus operandi for decades. The primary targets of such International miscreants were capitalist and pro-American businesses, assets, military and political figures. Always in need of funds, these arch-criminals were not above robbing banks and armored cars or engaging in outright extortion.

In case your memory has faded, some of these "Communist Revolutionaries" sought to further their cause by tossing grenades into a packed movie theatre. They walked into Rome International Airport and opened fire on waiting passengers with submachine-guns. The people's champions detonated a bomb in front of the USO club in Naples, Italy.

One of their star players, Ilich Ramirez Sanchez, AKA "Carlos the Jackal" was, among other things, credited with lobbing grenades into a Paris café, killing and maiming people as they ate. This is representative of the tactics used by those who fought for the oppressed workers of the world.

Although separated by nationality and distance, the anti-capitalist terrorist groups had a common thread, Marxist ideology and the backing of the Soviet Union and its puppet states. Through the KGB (the Committee for State Security), the Soviets provided funding, training and, when necessary, safe haven for terrorists all across the globe during the historical era we now call the Cold War years.

Premiers Khrushchev, Brezhnev, Andropov, and Gorbachev did not need to send divisions of troops into West Germany, Italy, France, Greece, Belgium, or Spain in their attempt to de-stabilize the capitalist West and the allies of the United States. The Soviet bosses had hundreds, if not thousands, of willing minions to do their dirty work and execute acts of extreme violence, all in the name of the "People's Revolution."

Terrorist support cells littered the European continent and training camps were found in the more unlikely locations of Cuba and Africa. The sad truth is that the West paid too little attention to what went on in the African continent and Marxism was allowed to flourish. Soviet supported dictators worked their way to the heads of several nations by armed revolt or the threat of the same.

So, where are the Communist Revolutionaries today, those idealistic soldiers of the worldwide People's Army? They are gone. Yes, once in a while we hear a peep from a one of the people's soldiers who has not yet gotten the memo "Communism is dead." Where are these communist freedom fighters? They are either dead, rotting in jail, or hiding. How did this come about? Evolution? Fate? Bad luck?

The Defeat of the Red Terrorist

Without wishing to oversimplify the matter, Communist backed terrorism was defeated through a combined effort of three entities: Military Force, Intelligence Gathering, and Law Enforcement. No, holding hands, burning incense, and singing "Kum Ba Yah" were not a part of the success plan.

Though listed last, law enforcement will be addressed first, primarily because standard civilian law enforcement is the least effective way to combat organized terrorism, especially that which is backed by a sponsor state. Many countries learned early on that capturing and imprisoning members of terrorist cells only led to further terrorism inspired to secure the release of their comrades. This was one of several reasons that Israel adopted a "no negotiation" stance when dealing with terrorists.

Civilian police agencies are not set up to handle the para-military threat that terrorists present. Police agencies investigate criminal activity, arrest suspects, and aid in the prosecution thereof. The truth is; most police work is reactive, not proactive. Cops show up after the crime and try to catch and jail the criminal. When dealing with military-style assaults, random bombings, and assassination, most civilian police agencies do not have the resources or experience to handle the task. It was for these reasons that special anti-terrorist agencies were formed and trained.

The British SAS, the German GSG-9, the French GIGN, the American Special Forces Detachment Delta, and other such units were tasked with handling organized terrorists the way a military commando organization would, not like your local police patrolman. It is true, nonetheless, that anti-terrorist teams have often reacted to crimes such as kidnapping and hostage situations.

The counter-terrorist forces are infinitely better trained to handle such operations than a typical law enforcement agency or even the conventional military. The capture of live terrorists is valuable from an intelligence standpoint. However, it can be effectively argued that no terrorist group ever hijacked a plane to free their comrades from the morgue.

Strong intelligence gathering provides the military arm with targets and prospective targets. Such intelligence gives the good guys a place to start looking when a kidnapping occurs, and suspects to round up after a group has claimed responsibility for an attack. Your intelligence arm gives you vital information to support your anti-terrorist activities and positive propaganda for the people at home.

Once located, terrorist strongholds, training camps, and hiding places can be effectively neutralized with swift and determined military force. Unfortunately, as long as there is a sponsor state to provide money, material, and cover for terrorist organizations, they will continue to flourish.

Law enforcement and intelligence agencies continued to check the communist terrorists throughout the 1970's and 1980's, however, it was not until the fall of the Soviet Union that these terror cells crumbled and ceased to be serious players on the world stage.

The game of terrorism is an expensive one. You must have a steady flow of cash, training for new members, and someone with enough clout to hide you when the good guys are looking for you. Sure, you can run off and hide in the mountains or jungles, but you cannot effectively strike your targets unless you are among them.

While there were a number of factors that led to the defeat of Soviet Communism and the end of the Cold War, it cannot be denied that our strong military, and the resolve to use it if necessary, was one of the most important factors. The resolve of President Ronald Reagan, British Prime Minister Margaret Thatcher and their allies halted the Soviet expansion and forced them to collapse under their own weight.

Terrorism in the 21st Century

The terrorists we face today are just as fanatical as those of the Cold War era, if not more so. They are driven by a zealous hatred of freedom and western civilization.   Like those before them, Islamic terrorists have as their goal the destabilization of a free, democratic world led, naturally, by the United States. They would have us withdraw all of our interests from the rest of the world and hide behind our borders giving them free reign over all they can get their hands on.

As I sit to pen this piece, the United States Military and elite anti-terrorist units worldwide have attempted to keep Islamic terrorists in check. Sadly, the reality of the situation in 2014 is that political expediency has trumped determined action and effective resolution. The

United States Military has been hampered for greater than five years by "Rules of Engagement" that are prima facie in favor of the enemy and work directly against the effort to actually win the war.

Unfortunately, the Muslim terrorists are far from giving in. With a series of well-planned attacks, terrorists were able to disrupt an election in Spain and cause the installation of a weak, appeasing government in that country.

Islamofascists have attacked embassies and consulates abroad with little to no repercussions. We have seen innocent civilians butchered in shopping malls and elsewhere. Terrorists tend to be imitative rather than innovative. If something works for them, they will keep on doing it as long as they can get away with it.

Even more recently, the massacre of children at a school in Russia has shown that there is no depth of depravity or horror that they are not willing to sink to. We are dealing with an enemy who can mentally justify the torture and murder of children. Think on that for a moment.

United States politicians and their willing accomplices in the media have pretended that

Islamic radicals were on the run or marginalized to the point where they could no longer be considered a threat. Though we had been making great strides towards reducing the number of terrorists and their ability to wage war against us, it will not be until their sponsors are defeated that the Islamic terrorists will become as impotent as their communist brothers.

Arresting or killing the current leadership of these groups will not win the current war against terrorism. Yes, they will be weakened by our actions, but as long as there are countries willing to train, support, and harbor terrorists there will still be terrorists willing to die for their cause.

When Islamic terrorists have no country to hide in, no sponsor state to train and equip them, and no Swiss bank accounts to fund them, they will crumble. Do not fall prey to the desire for a quick fix. This war cannot be won after one or two battles. Citizens need to steel themselves with the understanding that it will take many years to put an end to this danger. The Cold War and state sponsored Communist Terror lasted for decades.

Consider this; the 1961 erection of the Berlin Wall was one harbinger of things to come, as was the 1966 Tri-Continental Conference in Havana, Cuba. During this international meeting, the Soviet Union and their puppet Fidel Castro pledged to aid and support all Anti-Capitalist Revolutionaries. When Mikhail Gorbachev resigned in 1991 this was effectively the end of the Soviet Union and their ability to provide continued support to terrorists.

My point is this, accepting that the Cold War era was in effect from 1961 to Gorbachev's resignation in 1991, it took a full thirty years to defeat that particular threat to freedom and democracy. Our current war against Islamic extremism was working until we decided that it was no longer a war but a police action and that we needed to rebuild the enemy's homeland before the enemy was defeated. It will take many years more of serious and determined effort to bring it under control. It is unrealistic for citizens of the United States to expect a quick end to this threat.

Mistakes Made

When terrorists struck hard on our shores at the World Trade Center in 1993, we mistakenly tried to treat it as a law enforcement issue. We deceived ourselves into thinking that capturing and jailing a few terrorists was a viable solution to the problem. Like a dormant cancer, Islamic terrorists within the United States went into submission after the conviction of their brothers for the first Trade Center bombing. They literally took years to plan and organize their next big move.

Do not forget, prior to 9/11/01, Islamic Terrorists struck us repeatedly. They attacked the USS Cole, killing numerous sailors. They bombed our embassies in Africa and they blew up U.S. military housing in Saudi Arabia. Each time we were attacked we reacted and treated the attack as a single incident, not a coordinated war against us. We vowed to find and arrest those responsible, but we failed to declare war against Islamofascism as a whole. They had declared war on us. However, we were too slow to understand that fact and paid for it on September 11, 2001.

The terrorist cancer is back and more acute than ever before. We are left with no other alternative than complete surgery to remove the rotten tissue of terrorism from the world body. Failing to do so will result in the slow, painful, and certain death of freedom, not only for the United States, but freedom loving people everywhere.

A Game Plan

How do you defeat an enemy that is willing to die for his or her cause? A good friend of mine is a former Marine Corps Sniper and an active executive protection agent. Recently, a gentleman who was genuinely troubled by the threat of Islamic fanatics posed the previous question to him. The former Marine Sniper responded. "When confronted with such an individual, I try to seek an open mind." "How is that?" The man asked seriously. "Well, you see, I have found that a well-placed .308 round tends to open their mind right up." My friend answered. He was not joking.

How can we hope to defeat terrorists in the 21st Century? It begins with a commitment from every freedom-loving citizen to accept the fact that there is evil in the world and that evil needs to be stopped. You must support leaders who are determined to destroy that evil, not negotiate with it. You must hold weak-willed and spineless politicians accountable for their actions and non-actions.

This enemy cannot be negotiated with. A truce to a terrorist is just extra time to strengthen their positions and prepare for the next attack. How can you negotiate with someone who is willing to torture and murder a child? Or take a knife and saw the head off of an innocent hostage to make their point?

Our law enforcement and military must seek out and destroy the enemy wherever they are hiding, even within our own borders. Any country or leader who trains, supplies, or harbors terrorists must be put on notice that their time is short. Like the "People's Revolutionaries" who came before them, as long as today's terrorists have a home, a support system, and a place to hide, they will never stop.

When will the war against the terrorists be over? It will be over when there is no one left to give them guns and money, when there are no more parades in downtown Tehran or Damascus to honor their vicious deeds, and when there is no place on earth left for them to hide.

Conclusion

It should be obvious to you at this point that this undertaking is not going to happen overnight, over a weekend or even a month or two. I could use the old quote about the journey of a thousand miles, but you should already get the gist.

Many of you who read this may have already begun and that is a big positive. If you are just now standing at the starting line it is time to get going. There is no time like the present. You bought this book and read it because you absolutely had the feeling that you could and should be doing more than you were.

It is my most sincere hope that the words contained herein have somehow inspired and motivated you. That is the focus of the Patriot Fire Team, to inspire and motivate each other. The moral support and peer affirmation you get from like-minded patriots is not something you can buy at a gun show or order online and that is what makes these qualities so precious.

No one can tell you what the future has in store for the United States of America. I can, however, tell you this with certainty. The success or failure of this nation has not so much to do with who sits in the halls of the state and national capitals as it does with those who put them there.

The abdication of power by the legitimate citizen and the disinterest of the common man has and will always lead to tyrannical behavior on the part of the "public servant." If the people do not cling jealously to the authority guaranteed them by the founding documents, why should the self-appointed ruling class struggle to remind them of their rights?

Words written on parchment two centuries ago have only the strength and power of the living generation. This generation must not only take the time to understand those words, but actively fight for their preservation. We do not need to rewrite the playbook, we simply need to read it and follow the guidelines we have been blessed by providence to possess.

References

"Motivation and Personality" Abraham Harold Maslow, Robert Freger, Harper and Rowe, 1987

"Relief Workers Confront 'Urban Warfare': Violence disrupts evacuation, relief efforts in New Orleans" CNN.com September 1, 2005

"The Political Thought of the American Revolution", Clinton Rossiter, Harcourt, Brace & World, Inc. 1953

Bill of Rights, United States Constitution, 1791

"Efficiency of the Militia Act" H.R. 11645 U.S. Library of Congress, 1902

"Paul Revere's Ride" David Hackett Fischer, Oxford University Press, 1995

Warren v. District of Columbia, US Supreme Court No. 02-7120

Guns Across the Border, Mike Detty, SkyHorse Publishing, 2013

About the Author

Paul G. Markel has worn many hats during his lifetime. He has been a U.S. Marine, Police Officer, Professional Bodyguard, and Small Arms and Tactics Instructor. Mr. Markel has been writing professionally for law enforcement and firearms periodicals for twenty plus with hundreds upon hundreds of articles and several books in print.

Paul is the host and producer of Student of the Gun TV and Radio. Mr. Markel is also the founder of Student of the Gun University, an entity dedicated to education and enlightenment.

"Professor Paul" has been teaching safe and effective firearms handling to students young and old for decades and has worked actively with the 4H Shooting Sports program. Paul holds numerous instructor certifications in multiple disciplines; nonetheless, he is and will remain a dedicated Student of the Gun.

Ready for danger; soft armor, pistol, light, phone, and TQ

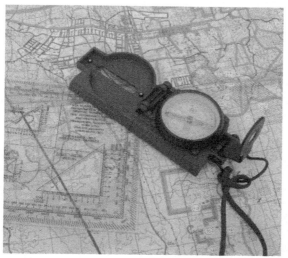

Photo Descriptions

Page 233   Suede Desert boots (top) Tradition Black Leather (Bottom)

Page 234   Light Weight Assault boots (top) Comfortable, Quality Socks (bottom)

Page 235   Poncho liner, Sleeping pad, and Sleeping bag (top) Shemaghs (bottom)

Page 236   Quality Backpack (top), Lensatic compass and maps (bottom)

Page 237   New Orleans, La. post-Katrina (top), Author's Gear in N.O. post-Katrina.

Page 238   Author with his team, USS Forrestal, 1989 (top), Author on Kuwaiti border, 1991 (bottom)

Page 239   Author, jungle patrol, Okinawa 1990

Additional Books by the Author

Student of the Gun: A Beginner Once, A Student for Life

Faith and the Patriot: A Belief Worth Fighting For

Team Honey Badger: Raising Fearless Kids is a Cowardly World

The Intolerant Christian: Examining the Persecution of Faithful Christians in the United States of America